DATE DUE

DEMCO 38-296

DEMCO

THE
HISTORY
OF
ISSUES

Euthanasia

THE
HISTORY
OF
ISSUES

Euthanasia

Loreta M. Medina, *Book Editor*

Bruce Glassman, *Vice President*
Bonnie Szumski, *Publisher*
Helen Cothran, *Managing Editor*

GREENHAVEN PRESS
An imprint of Thomson Gale, a part of The Thomson Corporation

THOMSON
—— ✳ ——™
GALE

Detroit • New York • San Francisco • San Diego • New Haven, Conn.
Waterville, Maine • London • Munich

For more information, contact
Greenhaven Press
27500 Drake Rd.
Farmington Hills, MI 48331-3535
Or you can visit our Internet site at http://www.gale.com

Cover credit: © Bob Croslin/CORBIS

LIBRARY OF CONGRESS CATALOGING-IN-PUBLICATION DATA

Euthanasia / Loreta M. Medina, book editor.
    p. cm. — (The history of issues)
Includes bibliographical references and index.
ISBN 0-7377-2005-0 (lib. : alk. paper) — ISBN 0-7377-2006-9 (pbk. : alk. paper)
    1. Euthanasia—History. 2. Euthanasia—Moral and ethical aspects.
3. Euthanasia—Law and legislation—History. 4. Assisted suicide—Moral and ethical aspects. I. Medina, Loreta M. II. Series.
R726.E77582 2005
179.7—dc22
                                                                    2004040501

Printed in the United States of America

Contents

Chapter 1: Euthanasia and Suicide in Ancient and Modern Times

Chapter 2: Legal Battles

Chapter 3: The Ethical Debate

had their lives ended without their consent by physicians.

Chapter 4: Physicians and Assisted Suicide

ing, dying patients. However, when palliative care fails to stop agonizing pain, physician-assisted suicide should be a legal choice.

Foreword

In the 1940s, at the height of the Holocaust, Jews struggled to create a nation of their own in Palestine, a region of the Middle East that at the time was controlled by Britain. The British had placed limits on Jewish immigration to Palestine, hampering efforts to provide refuge to Jews fleeing the Holocaust. In response to this and other British policies, an underground Jewish resistance group called Irgun began carrying out terrorist attacks against British targets in Palestine, including immigration, intelligence, and police offices. Most famously, the group bombed the King David Hotel in Jerusalem, the site of a British military headquarters. Although the British were warned well in advance of the attack, they failed to evacuate the building. As a result, ninety-one people were killed (including fifteen Jews) and forty-five were injured.

Early in the twentieth century, Ireland, which had long been under British rule, was split into two countries. The south, populated mostly by Catholics, eventually achieved independence and became the Republic of Ireland. Northern Ireland, mostly Protestant, remained under British control. Catholics in both the north and south opposed British control of the north, and the Irish Republican Army (IRA) sought unification of Ireland as an independent nation. In 1969, the IRA split into two factions. A new radical wing, the Provisional IRA, was created and soon undertook numerous terrorist bombings and killings throughout Northern Ireland, the Republic of Ireland, and even in England. One of its most notorious attacks was the 1974 bombing of a Birmingham, England, bar that killed nineteen people.

In the mid-1990s, an Islamic terrorist group called al Qaeda began carrying out terrorist attacks against American targets overseas. In communications to the media, the organization listed several complaints against the United States. It generally opposed all U.S. involvement and presence in the Middle East. It particularly objected to the presence of U.S. troops in Saudi Arabia, which is the home of several Islamic holy sites. And it strongly condemned the United States for supporting the nation of Israel, which it claimed was an oppressor of Muslims. In 1998 al Qaeda's leaders issued a fatwa (a religious legal statement) calling for Muslims to kill Americans. Al Qaeda acted on this order many times—most memorably on September 11, 2001, when it attacked the World Trade Center and the Pentagon, killing nearly three thousand people.

These three groups—Irgun, the Provisional IRA, and al Qaeda—have achieved varied results. Irgun's terror campaign contributed to Britain's decision to pull out of Palestine and to support the creation of Israel in 1948. The Provisional IRA's tactics kept pressure on the British, but they also alienated many would-be supporters of independence for Northern Ireland. Al Qaeda's attacks provoked a strong U.S. military response but did not lessen America's involvement in the Middle East nor weaken its support of Israel. Despite these different results, the means and goals of these groups were similar. Although they emerged in different parts of the world during different eras and in support of different causes, all three had one thing in common: They all used clandestine violence to undermine a government they deemed oppressive or illegitimate.

The destruction of oppressive governments is not the only goal of terrorism. For example, terror is also used to minimize dissent in totalitarian regimes and to promote extreme ideologies. However, throughout history the motivations of terrorists have been remarkably similar, proving the old adage that "the more things change, the more they remain the same." Arguments for and against terrorism thus boil down to the same set of universal arguments regardless of the age: Some argue that terrorism is justified to change (or, in the case of state terror, to maintain) the prevailing political order; others respond that terrorism is inhumane and unacceptable under any circumstances. These basic views transcend time and place.

Similar fundamental arguments apply to other controversial social issues. For instance, arguments over the death penalty have always featured competing views of justice. Scholars cite biblical texts to claim that a person who takes a life must forfeit his or her life, while others cite religious doctrine to support their view that only God can take a human life. These arguments have remained essentially the same throughout the centuries. Likewise, the debate over euthanasia has persisted throughout the history of Western civilization. Supporters argue that it is compassionate to end the suffering of the dying by hastening their impending death; opponents insist that it is society's duty to make the dying as comfortable as possible as death takes its natural course.

Greenhaven Press's The History of Issues series illustrates this constancy of arguments surrounding major social issues. Each volume in the series focuses on one issue—including terrorism, the death penalty, and euthanasia—and examines how the debates have both evolved and remained essentially the same over the years. Primary documents such as newspaper articles, speeches, and government reports illuminate historical developments and offer perspectives from throughout history. Secondary sources provide overviews and commentaries from a more contemporary perspective. An introduction begins each anthology and supplies essential context and background. An annotated table of contents, chronology, and index allow for easy reference, and a bibliography and list of organizations to contact point to additional sources of information on the book's topic. With these features, The History of Issues series permits readers to glimpse both the historical and contemporary dimensions of humanity's most pressing and controversial social issues.

Introduction

The word *euthanasia* means deliberately killing or permitting the death of hopelessly sick or injured individuals with the intention of relieving their suffering. People use a variety of terms to describe euthanasia, including "mercy killing," "assisted suicide," and "physician-assisted suicide." Euthanasia can also be passive or active. Passive euthanasia involves an incurably ill person refusing or asking for the withdrawal of life-sustaining medical support. Passive euthanasia also refers to cases in which a doctor prescribes painkilling drugs knowing that a terminally ill patient may choose to overdose on them and die. Active euthanasia takes place when a person deliberately causes the death of a terminally ill individual—for instance, when a person gives a dying parent a lethal injection. Finally, euthanasia can be voluntary or involuntary. Voluntary euthanasia is euthanasia with the consent of the dying person; involuntary euthanasia is performed without an individual's consent. For many centuries advocates and critics of euthanasia have engaged in a heated debate over the morality of the practice. Although the central debate has always been about whether humans have the right to end a life that many believe is bestowed by God, changes in social values and political institutions have shifted the focus of the debate over time.

Mercy Killing in the Early Twentieth Century

During the early decades of the twentieth century, the word *euthanasia* was equated with mercy killing. Advocates believed that people suffering from intolerable physical and psychological pain should be allowed or helped to die for their own good. In a 1937 poll 46 percent of respondents favored physician-assisted suicide for terminally ill patients if the patients and their families requested it. However, euthanasia was still illegal and many people accused of assisting with suicide had to go to court. Historian Ian Dowbiggin describes some of these cases:

> The euthanasia movement received invaluable publicity from the frequent press reports of mercy-killing trials during the 1930s. These cases often featured desperate parents killing their handicapped children, or spouses putting their chronically-ill loved ones to death. Some defendants were acquitted, some given prison sentences, and others committed to mental hospitals. In most instances, there was no clear evidence that the victims had requested euthanasia formally. In other instances, individuals wracked with pain begged to be put out of their misery.[1]

In 1938 the Euthanasia Society of America (ESA) was established in New York. Its goal was to make euthanasia legal in the United States. However, its members also promoted the mass sterilization of prison inmates and the "mercy killing" of the mentally handicapped.

The Nazi "Euthanasia" Campaign

After World War II, news reached America of the horrific killings committed by the Nazis under the guise of euthanasia. The Nazi campaign, begun in 1934, aimed to produce a superior Aryan race by preventing the mentally handicapped from reproducing. It resulted in the forcible sterilization of three hundred thousand to four hundred thousand people. In 1939 the sterilization program evolved into a more elaborate euthanasia program to kill the physically and mentally handicapped. From 1930 to 1945 the Nazis carried out a euthanasia campaign that killed more than two hundred thousand people, including children and the elderly.

The Nazi killings caused a decline in the promotion of euthanasia in the United States. By 1947 support for euthanasia had fallen to 37 percent. The Euthanasia Society's campaign for the legalization of euthanasia faltered.

Modern Technology Reopens the Debate over Euthanasia

The euthanasia campaign and the accompanying debate were renewed in the United States toward the beginning of the 1950s as the field of medicine underwent astonishing change. Vaccines, antibiotics, medical equipment, and other inventions armed doctors with new tools to battle disease and prolong life. The newfound power of medicine to delay death led to some weakening of religious faith and the strengthening of a secular outlook. In the minds of many sick patients and their families, God was no longer the sole arbiter of death; human intervention could delay it. Doctors thus became "saviors" and "miracle workers" who could prolong life as well as help suffering patients die.

The euthanasia movement was further strengthened by a statement made by Pope Pius XII in 1957 that made passive euthanasia acceptable to the Catholic Church. The pontiff announced that the Catholic Church condoned a patient's refusal of extraordinary treatment when death was imminent and further medical treatment would only prolong agony. The church also allowed the use of painkillers that could threaten a patient's life, as long as they were not prescribed with the intention of ending life. For euthanasia proponents, the statement was a milestone: The church had sanctioned the limited use of euthanasia. Dowbiggin claims that the pope's declaration improved relations between proponents and critics of euthanasia: "In a single stroke, the Pope helped to alter the terrain beneath the entire debate over euthanasia, making a constructive dialogue possible among those concerned about medical care for the dying and ending the standoff between the ESA and its opponents."[2]

In the 1960s the debate over euthanasia gained more momentum with the birth of the civil rights movement. At the start of the decade, black students in the South were waging a campaign to end racial segregation. They launched sit-ins, street demonstrations, and other mass actions that eventually led to the desegregation of buses, terminals, stores, restaurants, and other public facilities. The students would later help organize the 1963 March on Washington, which was instrumental in bringing about successful civil rights legislation and changing the political landscape of the United States. Successes in the civil rights movement inspired students to press for other goals, including the end of the Cold War, peace in Vietnam, and the abolition of the death penalty.

Widespread activism in the 1960s led to the transformation of the health care system in the following decade as people extended ideas about civil rights to include the right to refuse medical treatment. In 1973 the American Hospital Association formulated a Patient's Bill of Rights, which included the right to be fully informed of the details of their medical treatment, as well as the right to decline treatment. This refusal of medical treatment was a form of passive euthanasia. Advocates of euthanasia viewed the Patient's Bill of Rights as a small triumph and pressed forward with their public campaign to legalize euthanasia.

The Right to Die

In the 1970s supporters of euthanasia began to use the term "the right to die" to describe their belief that seriously ill or injured patients or their families should be allowed to discontinue life support when there is no hope of recovery. The 1976 case of Karen Ann Quinlan in New Jersey dramatically illustrates some of the issues involved in this crusade for the right to die. At the age of twenty-one, Karen fell into a coma after taking drugs and alcohol. Only a respirator and feeding tube kept her alive. Her parents eventually concluded that she would never come out of her coma and asked the hospital to remove the respirator to let her die. The hospital, a large Catholic facility, refused the request, prompting a court case. In 1976 the New Jersey Supreme Court finally ruled that the Quinlans had the right to have the respirator removed.

The *Quinlan* case was historic in that it marked the first time that a state supreme court ruled that the state has no right to force a person to remain on life-supporting devices. For supporters of euthanasia the ruling in the *Quinlan* case, which established a legal precedent for passive euthanasia, was a positive step toward their goal of legalizing euthanasia.

The *Quinlan* case was also important because it brought into focus the issue of the rights of an incompetent patient. The courts repeatedly questioned whether Karen Quinlan would have wanted her life support removed. According to her family, she had stated while she was still healthy and competent that she never would wish to live as a vegetable, dependent on machines for all her bodily functions. According to the courts, such an expressed wish constitutes a patient's consent. The *Quinlan* case also popularized the use of living wills, which are advance instructions in which patients describe the medical treatment they would refuse if they became incompetent. Living wills provide guidelines to families and the hospital staff about whether to continue or withdraw life-prolonging treatment for the terminally ill. With evidence of an individual's wishes, a court can decide in favor of a patient's family who wants to withdraw life support. In 1976 California passed the nation's first law sanctioning living wills; in the next decade, thirty-six states enacted similar laws.

The Hemlock Society Campaigns to Legalize Euthanasia

The euthanasia movement seized the opportunities created by the *Quinlan* case to move forward. In the 1980s advocates of euthanasia brought the debate to the doorstep of state voters. They sought to bring the matter to the American public and ask them to take action through voter initiatives. The campaign was led by a British journalist,

Derek Humphry. After assisting in the suicide of his terminally ill wife in London in 1975, he moved to California, where he believed a campaign to legalize euthanasia would have a chance of succeeding.

Before launching ballot initiatives, Humphry started out with an information campaign, publishing books, appearing on television and radio talk shows, and giving seminars to promote euthanasia. He approached his crusade with daring by publishing guides describing how to commit or assist in suicide. His books include *Jean's Way*, which describes how he helped his wife die, and *Let Me Die Before I Wake*, a manual on using drugs to commit suicide. A much later book, *Final Exit* (1991), surpasses his earlier books in its audacity. It contains explicit instructions on how to commit suicide, including drug dosage tables.

In 1980 Humphry and his second wife, Ann Wickett, established the Hemlock Society, which in Humphry's words is "America's first group to fight exclusively to change the law on assisted suicide."[3] The society faced a formidable task as many states at the time considered assisted suicide as murder or manslaughter. However, supporters of legalized euthanasia argued that a dying person should be able to choose euthanasia to achieve "dignity at the end of life." In 1986 the Hemlock Society drafted a law on voluntary euthanasia and physician-assisted suicide that limited the procedure to the terminally ill and required patient competence and consent. In the following years the society launched three ballot initiatives to legalize voluntary euthanasia and physician-assisted suicide (two in California and one in Washington), but all failed. Although the first ballot initiatives were rejected by voters, the work of the Hemlock Society and its supporters played a key role in increasing public awareness about the issue of euthanasia.

Active Euthanasia Becomes the Focus

In the 1990s the debate over euthanasia began to focus on issues of active euthanasia and physician-assisted suicide.

The man who almost single-handedly brought these issues to public attention was Jack Kevorkian, a retired pathologist. In the late 1980s he assisted in the suicides of several people who came to him for help. On many occasions he appeared on television, promoting a machine he had created that enabled a person to inject lethal drugs for the purpose of suicide. Michigan suspended his medical license in 1991 due to his assistance with suicides. Nonetheless, after the suspension halted his access to lethal prescription drugs, Kevorkian used carbon monoxide to assist in the suicides of several more people. Kevorkian, who frequently made headlines, eventually claimed he had helped between 130 and 150 people to die.

To many observers, what distinguished Kevorkian from most right-to-die advocates was, according to Dowbiggin, his belief in "euthanasia on demand, provided by doctors without government regulation, for both mentally competent and incompetent patients."[4] He also departed from the guiding principles of the euthanasia movement by agreeing to help people who were not terminally ill and people who had no signs of physical disease but were instead suffering from depression. Also, he did not know his patients well, nor did he have any long-term care relationships with them. These features of Kevorkian's practice alienated both euthanasia supporters and critics.

After dodging prosecution for several years, Kevorkian was finally convicted of murder in 1998 by a Michigan court. Thomas Youk, who was suffering from Lou Gehrig's disease (amyotrophic lateral sclerosis), had sought Kevorkian's help to end his life. Kevorkian videotaped his meeting with Youk. The tape showing Kevorkian administering lethal drugs to the man was broadcast on the CBS news show *60 Minutes* and became the pivotal piece of evidence that led to Kevorkian's conviction.

The issue of physician-assisted suicide finally made its way to the Supreme Court. In 1997 the Court ruled that the Constitution does not guarantee Americans the right to commit suicide with the help of a physician. This ruling upheld laws criminalizing physician-assisted suicide in New York and Washington, which had each been sued by physicians and patients arguing for the right to assisted suicide. The plaintiffs in both states claimed that the ban violated the Constitution's equal protection clause, which states that each and every citizen should enjoy the same rights, irrespective of economic status, social standing, ethnicity, gender, and other factors. The plaintiffs in New York and Washington maintained that prohibiting injured, suffering individuals or the terminally ill from getting a physician's help in committing suicide discriminates against them, violating their "right to die." The attornies for the plaintiffs further argued that the prohibition against assisted suicide particularly discriminates against those people suffering from intolerable pain who are not in a hospital setting and therefore do not have ready access to a physician's help or painkilling drugs.

The Supreme Court acknowledged constitutional protection in allowing a competent patient to request termination of medical treatment, but refused to extend this protection to assisted suicide. The Court disagreed with the attornies' argument that removing life support is the same as providing painkillers to end a life. The Court maintained that the first case involves letting a patient die while the second involves actively ending a patient's life. The Court also deliberately left it to the state legislatures to decide whether to legalize physician-assisted suicide.

Oregon Legalizes Physician-Assisted Suicide

In 1997 while the Washington and New York cases were being tried, euthanasia advocates achieved their greatest victory: The state of Oregon finally secured a court ruling to enforce its 1994 Death with Dignity Act legalizing physician-assisted suicide. According to the act, physicians can assist in suicide only if the patient is terminally ill and has given consent, if the procedure is the last resort, and if an independent physician has confirmed the procedure's necessity.

Oregon's law was enacted more than fifty years after the Euthanasia Society was established in 1938. Advocates celebrated, but the euphoria was short-lived. In 2001 Attorney General John Ashcroft posed a new challenge to Oregon's law, warning that physicians who dispensed lethal drugs to end a life would be prosecuted. Today the matter is still being resolved by the courts.

Meanwhile, other states have attempted to follow Oregon's lead. In 1998 Michigan carried out a ballot initiative, but it was rejected by voters. In 2000 Maine also held a ballot initiative, but it too was rejected. Because of the hurdles that Oregon continues to face and the failure of recent ballot initiatives, observers do not predict an easy road ahead for the euthanasia movement. They note that while Americans say they favor physician-assisted suicide when polled, they waver when confronted with the issue more directly through ballot initiatives. This hesitation to legalize active euthanasia after decades of debate reveals how deeply contentious the issue remains. The question of whether humans have the right to end a life will never be easy to resolve.

Notes

1. Ian Dowbiggin, *A Merciful End: The Euthansia Movement in Modern America.* New York: Oxford University Press, 2003, p. 34.
2. Dowbiggin, *A Merciful End*, p. 98.
3. Quoted in Carolyn S. Roberts and Martha Gorman, eds., *Euthanasia: A Reference Book.* Santa Barbara, CA: ABC-CLIO, 1996, p. 13.
4. Dowbiggin, *A Merciful End*, p. 166.

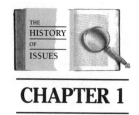

THE
HISTORY
OF
ISSUES

CHAPTER 1

Euthanasia and Suicide in Ancient and Modern Times

Chapter Preface

Today, as in the past, Christian teaching provides the basis for arguments against taking one's life and assisting others in ending their lives. Among the early proponents of the Christian prohibition against suicide and euthanasia was St. Augustine (A.D. 345–430), whose writings assert that killing oneself or another is immoral. Since God is the source of life, he reasoned, it is only God who can take back that life. In the thirteenth century, Thomas Aquinas echoed St. Augustine, declaring that the divine commandment against killing others also covers killing oneself.

Once the belief system took root in the Western world, the Christian objection to suicide became widespread and influenced church law and teaching. For centuries, Christianity's prohibition against suicide was entrenched. Gerald A. Larue of the Hemlock Society calls the antisuicide position the "heritage of the Christian Church and particularly the Roman Catholic Church."

In the United States, during the first half of the twentieth century, advocates of euthanasia had to contend with deep-seated religious beliefs in their initial attempts to promote and legalize euthanasia. In 1906 the first attempt in Ohio to introduce a bill to legalize euthanasia met with vast opposition.

Religion's hold was shaken in the 1950s by forces over which Christian churches had no power. Medical advances such as vaccines, antibiotics, modern equipment, and extraordinary procedures that prolong and save lives led to the awareness that God was no longer the sole arbiter of life and death. Instead, physicians and their tools were seen as the new saviors. It was in cognizance of this new reality that Pope Pius XII announced in 1957 that Catholics and their families did not have to continue "extraordinary treatments" in cases where the patient's death was imminent. Once the church leader had spoken, the debate on the subject of death opened up. Eventually, public opinion began to shift in favor of passive euthanasia, the refusal or withdrawal of life-sustaining treatment for terminally ill patients.

Today, while passive euthanasia has been secured as a right, the battle has shifted to the legalization of physician-assisted suicide. The Catholic Church, fundamentalist Christians, and other groups continue to oppose the practice on the grounds that it violates the sanctity of life and contradicts God's will.

Views on Euthanasia and Suicide from Ancient Greece to the Middle Ages

MICHAEL M. UHLMANN

In the following selection, Michael M. Uhlmann discusses the origins of Western thought on suicide. The author explains that the Greeks tolerated suicide, but in the fourth century B.C. the norm was challenged by a school associated with Hippocrates that forbade physicians to assist in suicide. The philosophers Aristotle and Plato also argued against assisted suicide. The early Christians adapted the Hippocratic teaching to their purposes. A key Christian philosopher, Saint Augustine, asserts in his works that the divine commandment against killing includes a prohibition against suicide. In the thirteenth century, the Christian view was further refined by Thomas Aquinas. Christian thought on suicide later would become so widespread that it would dominate the medical ethics of the Western world. At the time of writing, Michael M. Uhlmann was a senior fellow at the Ethics and Public Policy Center and a professor of government in the Washington program of Claremont McKenna College. He is currently a professor of political science at Claremont Graduate University. Uhlmann is the editor of Last Rights? Assisted Suicide and Euthanasia Debated.

Michael M. Uhlmann, *Last Rites? Assisted Suicide and Euthanasia Debated.* Grand Rapids, MI: William B. Eerdmans Publishing Company/Ethics and Public Policy Center, 1998. Copyright © 1998 by the Ethics and Public Policy Center. All rights reserved. Reproduced by permission.

Without question, the most powerful influence on Western thought about suicide is Christian theology, which originates in the Jewish Scriptures' account of the creation of man in God's image. By marking man's nature with a divine character, God intended not only to bestow upon human life a special dignity but to limit man's sovereignty over his own existence. That limitation is expressed, among other places, in the commandment "Thou shalt not kill," which affirms the goodness of life as a divine gift and God's abhorrence at the shedding of human blood.

Although this understanding first appeared in God's revelation to the Jews, and although Jewish law forbade suicide accordingly, the New Testament furnished the teaching with a new and universal dimension: belief in the mystery of the Incarnation—God become flesh through the union of divine and human nature in the person of Jesus Christ. With its affirmation of charity as man's highest duty and the promise of heavenly reward to those who die in God's grace, Christianity produced an optimism that was utterly alien to the prevailing ethos at the time of Christ's birth, indeed to any that had gone before. Here was a belief that, by giving an eternal dimension to suffering and death, also gave new meaning to life. God was no longer remote, impersonal, or indifferent: in taking human form, he showed his love for man through the redemptive act of Christ's death and resurrection, promising salvation to all who were faithful to his word. For the faithful Christian, death was no longer an end but the doorway to eternal life. . . .

The history of the Jews, significantly, is notable for the rarity of suicide, but among other peoples the practice seems to have been fairly widespread. Among the Greeks, for example, it was tolerated if not always formally approved, especially as a response to untreatable, painful illness or fear of ignominy. Early Greek physicians apparently felt little compunction about providing poisons to those who wished to end their lives. In the fourth century B.C., however, a school associated with the name of Hippocrates challenged the reigning medical orthodoxy by forbidding its members to assist others in the act of suicide. Although a distinctly minority view at the outset, the Hippocratic disposition grew in influence even before the rise of Christianity. In time, it was adapted to Christian purposes by the early Church Fathers and ultimately became the dominant medical ethic of the Western world. Hippocratic teaching on assisted suicide and euthanasia appears to have derived from the Pythagoreans, who held that human beings possessed immortal souls that were deemed to be pieces of fallen divinity. Although entombed in the body, the soul could be purified through the study of philosophy and mathematics and eventually liberated, thereafter migrating to its heavenly home.

Plato (427–347 B.C.)

Athough Pythagorean doctrine comes down to us mainly in fragments or by hearsay, its influence can be traced in a number of Platonic dialogues. The most important of these for our purposes is the *Phaedo*, which recounts a conversation between Socrates and a few friends during his last hours as he awaits execution. The *Phaedo* presents Plato's most elaborate discussion of the immortality of the soul and the implications of that belief for human behavior. In a brief exchange at the beginning of the dialogue, Socrates is asked to explain the absolute ban on suicide advocated by the Pythagoreans and other religious teachers, and to reconcile it with his own opinion that death may sometimes be preferable to life. Socrates restates what he understands the religious teaching to be: life is not ours to do with as we wilt because we have been placed in a kind of "prison" or "guard post" by the gods and are therefore not free to run away. He says that while this doctrine is not easy to understand, it does seem correct to him that the gods are our guardians and that we are but their possessions. . . .

The so-called suicide passage of the *Phaedo* is a brief introductory exchange in a longer work that argues for the philosophical life as the best way of life because it entails the perfection of a human being's highest part, his rational soul. Such a life necessarily requires a habituated detachment from bodily demands, so that the soul may partake more fully in the contemplation of that which is unchanging and eternal. Socrates contends that philosophy is in effect a lifelong practice in learning how to die; death is not to be feared but is to be welcomed as a release from the encumbrances of the body.

But if death is the gateway to unencumbered contemplation of the highest things, should it not be more hurriedly sought? Socrates makes no such argument. It is one thing, apparently, to welcome death when it comes and quite another thing to seek it actively. While Socrates does not flatly condemn suicide as always and everywhere immoral, he comes very close to that view. He grants to the act no general license, and least of all does he suggest or imply that it should be a matter of individual preference. His teaching seems to be that taking one's life would be morally acceptable if and only if one could be objectively certain that one's *soul* would be improved by the act. The general argument of the *Phaedo* indicates that such certainty is almost always beyond our grasp. Accordingly, we must, he says, "keep ourselves pure until god himself sets us free."

Some further light may be shed by a passage in the *Republic*, the dialogue in which Plato discusses the character of a political regime in accord with perfect justice. In the course of prescribing the best form of medicine for such a community, Socrates criticizes medical practice that prolongs life only through detailed regimens that consume virtually all of a patient's activity. A life utterly given over to bodily demands, Socrates implies, lacks a necessary condition for the virtuous life; and in cases where there is no prospect for recovery, it is better to cease treatment. Some read this passage as indicating Plato's support for suicide, at least for the incurably ill. But there are at least three reasons why this seems unlikely. First, Plato would have chosen an exceedingly roundabout way of making an argument about which he expressed strong doubt in the *Phaedo*. Second, withdrawing treatment and suicide are not always morally equivalent (in the case of withdrawal, death is caused by the underlying disease, not by the intentional act of patient or physician). Third, it must be noted that Socrates is here concerned not with suicide as such but with subjecting the medical art to the architectonic governance of philosophical wisdom. Taken in that context, the passing comment in the *Republic* appears to be little more than a confirmation of the general argument of the *Phaedo*—that undue preoccupation with the body can interfere with man's duty to perfect his soul.

A brief discussion of suicide also occurs in Plato's *Laws*, his effort to construct a regime that is informed by philosophical understanding while being only an imperfect rendition of the philosophically perfect political community sketched in the *Republic*. The dialogue is one of only a few in which someone other than Socrates is the philosophical protagonist. His place is taken by a nameless elder, referred to as the "Athenian Stranger.". . .

[The stranger declares that] those disposed to commit heinous crimes should be encouraged to purify themselves, sacrifice to the gods, and seek the company of virtuous men. If such steps are unavailing, the Stranger says that it would be better if those of incorrigible character "[departed] from this life."

This somewhat cryptic comment, which appears to be at odds with the teaching of the *Phaedo*, should be read in the light of a subsequent passage, where suicide is harshly condemned as a species of heinous crime in itself. There, one who commits suicide is to be accorded ignominious burial, on a par with those who murder members of their own family. In a word, the political community must be reminded that suicide is a grave offense against its good order and the wishes of the gods. Nevertheless, the Stranger adds that three classes of suicide should be spared such opprobrious treatment: (1) those who are forced to take their own lives subject to judicial decree (in the manner, for example, of Socrates); (2) those who are compelled by "some intolerable and inevitable misfortune;" and (3) those who find themselves in "some disgrace that is beyond remedy and endurance." Some read this passage as a movement away from the near-absolute disapprobation of suicide contained in the *Phaedo.* The Stranger, however, is here concerned with the amelioration of punishment rather than with the moral justification of suicide *per se.* Moreover, the actor in all three examples must be understood to be acting under some kind of powerful duress, whether legal, physical, social, or emotional. He does not act entirely as a free agent who is capable of making a rational choice; he is, so to speak, not himself. In the absence of such duress, death by his own hand is, and must be understood by others as, a species of "sloth and unmanly cowardice."

Aristotle (384–322 B.C.)

Plato's general condemnation of suicide is supported by his student Aristotle, who shares with his teacher the pre-eminent position at the head of the Western philosophical tradition. Together, their views constitute the foundation on which philosophers and theologians of the Christian era built their opposition to suicide, as modified by the light of biblical revelation. Whereas Plato's argument is subtle and at times paradoxical, Aristotle's is characteristically straightforward and more overtly didactic; and whereas Plato's is woven dialectically from discussions in three dialogues, Aristotle's must be gleaned from a few brief references in his *Nichomachean Ethics.*

In general, it may be said that Aristotle takes no exception to Plato's general condemnation of suicide. That may indeed explain why he is less interested in the question of suicide *per se* than in a generic question of which suicide is but an illustration: Is it possible to do oneself an injustice? His answer is regrettably brief and not easy to tease out. A few pages prior to this discussion, Aristotle has concluded that "no one can suffer injustice voluntarily, because no one can wish to be harmed." As a voluntary act, then, suicide cannot be unjust to the actor. The implication would seem to be that suicide is morally permissible.

Aristotle's argument, however, contains an additional element: though suicide may not be an injustice against oneself in a strict sense, the law nevertheless forbids it, and a just man will not contravene the law. . . . For [Aristotle], the law is not a collection of statutes designed to secure rights originating in some pre-political human condition, but an authoritative set of rules whose goal is to habituate citizens to a life of virtue. Because man is by nature a political animal, obedience to legal commands is an essential part of political justice, i.e., the obligation he owes to the political community. Although suicide may not be an injustice against oneself in the strict sense, it is, Aristotle says, an injustice against the political community whose existence is essential to one's own well-being.

Are we to infer, therefore, that in the absence of legal prohibition, Aristotle would have no objection to suicide? Or may suicide be morally objectionable in some other way? The only illustration Aristotle offers is that of a suicidal act committed in "a fit of passion." The implication is that suicide may be unjust not only because it contravenes the law, but also because it offends against the virtue of moderation. This reading is supported by a passage in Book III of the *Ethics*, during Aristotle's discussion of courage. Arguing that courage is the virtuous mean between cowardice and foolhardiness, he offers a number of examples, culminating in a description of the heroic soldier. Fearlessness in the face of death, particularly in combat, is the mark of a courageous man, but "to seek death in order to escape from poverty, or the pangs of love, or from pain and sorrow, is not the action of a courageous man, but rather of a coward; for it is weakness to fly from troubles, and the suicide does not endure death because it is noble to do so, but to escape from evil." This passage would seem to preclude justification of suicide on account of economic hardship, severe emotional distress, or physical infirmity—three of the most common justifications for "rational" suicide throughout the ages. . . .

The Stoics

Stoic ethical teaching mirrored Platonic beliefs in many respects—for example, that living well was in effect learning how to die, and that living well required the virtues of prudence, justice, courage, and moderation. But whereas for Plato the practice of virtue found its ultimate expression in the contemplative life, the Stoic wise man was honored less for his devotion to philosophy than for the calm resignation he brought to life's contingencies. . . .

As Professor John Finnis has pointed out, "the Stoic thesis . . . seems to be essentially an expression of piety directed toward a world-order whose order might well be regarded as not altogether admirable, and whose outcome might equally be regarded as a matter of indifference to us." There is nobility, certainly, in the Stoic understanding of virtue, which owes much to the thought of Plato and Aristotle, but it seems to lack a compelling sense of purpose. To borrow from Professor Finnis once again: "Boldly [the Stoic] will declare that, if you wish to compare one's choice of aim in life with a man aiming a spear at a target, then you must admit that the ultimate good, end, or aim that such a man has in view is *not* the target, *nor* the hitting of it, but the aiming it straight!" . . .

One ancient commentator articulated five separate grounds used by the Stoics to justify suicide. A thoughtful modern student of the subject has expanded the list to eight, which he divides roughly into two categories, "heroic" and "non-heroic." The heroic group includes the desire to escape shame and dishonor, to demonstrate total devotion to one's country, to end unrelieved grief over the death of a loved one, and to atone for the death one has accidentally dealt to another. In the non-heroic category are the desire to escape persistent and degrading poverty, to be reunited in death with a deceased loved one, to escape the boredom and futility of life, and to escape a relentlessly painful illness or injury. To consider this list is to realize at once how far we have come from the arguments of Plato and Aristotle—and how close we are to arguments commonly encountered in our own time. Indeed, it may be said that there is little in contemporary justifications for suicide that is not prefigured in some way in the various rationales furnished by the Stoics.

Augustine (354–420)

To turn from the writings of classical antiquity to those of Christianity is to experience a remarkable intellectual and psychological sea-change. Among the tasks facing early Christian thinkers was to explain their beliefs, insofar as possible, in terms that made sense among the then dominant philosophical schools. Few were more adept or forceful in this effort than St. Augustine of Hippo, the towering figure of the early Christian West, who remains a primary spiritual and intellectual inspiration for Christians in the twentieth century. . . .

Augustine's most extensive discussion of suicide is found in the opening sections of Book I of *The City of God.* Much of the first five books is directed against the fashionable accusation that Rome's decline and fall were directly proportional to the rise of Christianity. By orienting people to the service of a heavenly kingdom, so the argument went, Christianity had undermined Roman virtue and patriotism, which were grounded in citizen loyalty to the gods of the city. The gods of Rome had justly taken offense and, in anger, levied their revenge upon the city. If the Christian God were the one true God, Rome would not have been abandoned to the assault of the barbarians.

Augustine responds that, far from corrupting Rome,

Christian virtue had given new direction and vitality to a faltering and demonstrably debauched moral order. . . .

It is in this context that Augustine first addresses the question of suicide. He notes the case of certain Christian virgins who had been raped by the barbarian invaders and who had not avenged their defilement. The only virtuous course of action in such cases, pagan critics said, would have been to imitate the famous Roman noble-woman Lucretia, who assuaged the dishonor of her rape through suicide. . . . What kind of virtue is that? Augustine asks. We are forbidden by God to take the life of an innocent victim, but how is killing oneself any less an act of homicide? And how is it virtuous to compound one immoral act with another? An innocent victim has no valid ground for punishing herself; it would be as if she took upon herself the guilt of the perpetrator. . . .

The Bible, he says, rejects suicide, even for the sake of avoiding evil. The divine commandment against killing is general in nature and, he says, clearly includes suicide no less than homicide. True, he says, not all homicide is killing in the biblical sense; it is permissible, for example, to kill in obedience to a legitimate edict or in a just war—but suicide fits neither category. It is also true, Augustines concedes, that God appears to have given his specific approval to killing or suicide in certain rare instances recorded in the Bible: the command to Abraham, as a test of his faith, to slay Isaac, for example; and the command to Samson to pull down the temple, thereby killing himself as well as his captors. Such circumstances are exceptional, however, and the lesson to be drawn from them, Augustine argues, is not that Scripture is ambiguous in its teaching, but that homicide, whether of another or of oneself, is forbidden unless expressly sanctioned by divine command. . . .

Taken whole, Augustine's argument attempts to address the most common justifications for suicide that were offered during the early Christian era: the desire to avoid sin, to escape worldly troubles, to expiate guilt, to seek a better life, or to escape another's aggression. None of these, according to Augustine, can be squared with Christian teaching rightly understood. . . .

Augustine was not the first Christian thinker to argue against suicide, nor did he construct a Christian position out of thin air. He was the first, however, to set the argument down more or less systematically in one place, weaving it from pagan and scriptural sources alike to form what might be called the base-line Christian case against suicide. For centuries after his death, his argument exerted strong influence over the development of Western thought, customs, and law.

Thomas Aquinas (1225–1274)

From Augustine we move forward some 900 years, during which the Augustinian argument against suicide had become the reigning orthodoxy of Christendom. In the thirteenth century, the argument was refined and restated by Thomas Aquinas, who holds the premier position among Christian teachers of the Middle Ages. Like Augustine, he was at once a theologian, a philosopher, and a saint, who coursed masterfully over everything from cosmology and ontology to politics and ethics. And like Augustine, he drew upon both pagan and Christian sources, reconstituting them into a new synthesis that for many centuries after his death exerted an extraordinary influence. Whereas Augustine relied for the most part on neo-Platonic philosophical teaching, which he thought particularly congenial to Christian belief, Aquinas made abundant use of Aristotle. . . .

Whereas Aristotle neither knew of nor claimed any authority beyond human reason, Aquinas, as a devout Christian, acknowledged the existence of a supernatural order. The whole of the universe, natural and supernatural, is governed by "Divine Reason's conception of things," which Aquinas calls "eternal law." The eternal law is expressed both through explicit revelation (Scripture), which Aquinas calls "Divine law," and through natural law, which Aquinas defines as the participation of human reason in the eternal law. Explicit divine revelation, then, is not the only source of human wisdom. Moral truths can be established by means of reason alone. Of course, moral propositions are not always self-evident, but Aquinas would argue that with proper habituation and mature reflection, their truth can be established independently of any particular commandment of God. Taken together, these moral propositions constitute the natural law. In defining the natural law as the "rational creature's participation in the eternal law," Aquinas does not mean that its content is dictated by the specific divine instruction, but that, through reason, man can know and be bound by the moral order of the created universe.

With this by way of background, we are better able to appreciate Aquinas's treatment of suicide. In general, he concurs with Augustine on both theological and philosophical grounds and, indeed, begins his discussion by quoting from *The City of God*. Like Augustine, he specifically condemns suicide by virgins for the sake of protecting their chastity, and he agrees that the divine commandment against killing covers suicide no less than homicide. In short, suicide is always forbidden unless specifically commanded by God (as in the case of Samson). But while tracking the sense of Augustine's argument closely, Aquinas gives it a characteristically Thomistic twist by emphasizing certain features that were either understated or merely implicit in Augustine or not addressed at all by him. First, Aquinas argues—drawing on Aristotle—that it is in the nature of every living being to wish to preserve itself. To take one's own life is therefore not only a violation of God's commandment, but an act contrary to the natural law. Second, Aquinas emphasizes that suicide is an act of injustice against the political community. Here again he draws upon Aristotle in understanding political life as natural to man and essential to his well-being. No one is entitled to make rules for himself in disregard of the laws of the community, as if he were the solitary citizen and sole ruler of his own *polis*. Third, Aquinas condemns suicide as an arrogation of the power over life and death that rightly belongs to God alone. Man's sovereignty over himself, evidenced by his free will, does not extend to the manner of his passing from this world to the next.

Euthanasia from the Renaissance Through the Early Twentieth Century

DEREK HUMPHRY AND ANN WICKETT

In this article, Derek Humphry and Ann Wickett trace the history of beliefs about euthanasia from the Renaissance to the World War II era. They also describe the attempts of legislators in England and the United States to incorporate euthanasia into law. During the Renaissance, the medieval idea that suicide was an unforgivable sin against God gave way to the belief that each individual had to decide if suicide was the best solution in a given situation. The shift was brought about by rationalism, a philosophy that holds that reason is superior to belief in the supernatural. Michel de Montaigne, Francis Bacon, Thomas More, and other philosophers argued that alleviating suffering made suicide justifiable. By the eighteenth century some physicians claimed they should be able to help agonized patients have a "quick and painless" death. Humphry is a pioneer of the euthanasia movement in the United States. He and coauthor Ann Wickett established the Hemlock Society, which started the movement to legalize euthanasia. His books include Final Exit, Let Me Die Before I Wake, Jean's Way, *and* The Right to Die *(with Wickett). Wickett, Humphry's second wife, wrote* Double Exit, *a description*

Derek Humphry and Ann Wickett, *The Right to Die: Understanding Euthanasia.* New York: Harper & Row Publishers, Inc., 1986. Copyright © 1986 by Derek Humphry and Ann Wickett. All rights reserved. Reproduced by permission of the authors. For more information, see www.finalexit.org.

of the double suicide of her aging parents. Wickett herself committed suicide while suffering from depression.

With the revival of arts and letters in Europe in the fourteenth century, attitudes toward suicide changed radically. The Renaissance, a time of intense learning and scientific discovery, was beginning. A more worldly attitude meant that many superstitions and misconceptions were dispelled. In a sense, the world was turned on its axis. Educated opinion began to swing steadily away from the medieval condemnation of suicide. The movement continued and gathered momentum through the late 1600s and early 1700s.

With a reaffirmation of Greek and Roman values, the concept of an "easy death" gradually came to be regarded as an ideal once again. A sudden and intense strengthening of religious feeling in the fifteenth and sixteenth centuries was offset by a renewed enthusiasm for rationalism. Both the Catholic and the Protestant churches continued to condemn suicide, but most enlightened people no longer saw it as an inexpiable sin. As [French essayist Michel de] Montaigne observed: "The voluntariest death is the fairest."

In 1516, Sir Thomas More's *Utopia* was published. It depicted an ideal society in which voluntary euthanasia was officially sanctioned. Of terminal illness the noted Catholic wrote:

> If, besides being incurable, the disease also causes constant excruciating pain, some priests and government officials visit the person concerned and say. . . . Since your life's a misery to you, why hesitate to die? You're imprisoned in a torture chamber—why don't you break out and escape to a better world. . . . We'll arrange for your release. . . . If the patient finds these arguments convincing, he either starves himself to death, or is given a soporific and put painlessly out of his misery. But this is strictly voluntary.

What distinguished the sixteenth-century attitude toward

suicide from that of the Middle Ages was a reawakened interest in individualism. The shift in emphasis made the morality of life-and-death decisions more fluid and complex. Certainly, they were open to question. Montaigne, for instance, argued that man's dignity and ability to evaluate himself in the scale of nature made suicide justifiable. It was no disadvantage, in his eyes, if humanistic reflections of the period provided an opportunity to cast doubts on the teachings of the Church. Quite the contrary. With [Roman stoic Marcus Porcius] Cato as his model, he intended to restate Stoic ideas in his writings, tempered somewhat by a moderating Christianity. "Death," he wrote, "is a most assured haven, never to be feared, and often to be sought." And later he said: "All comes to one period, whether man make an end of himself, or whether he endure it. . . ."

The expansiveness of the Renaissance, then, not only enhanced man's sense of himself. It also, through scientific discovery, gave rise to innovative methods for treating disease. At the same time, efforts to keep patients alive often caused suffering—which threatened to diminish the value of life. [English philosopher Francis] Bacon, Montaigne, More, and [English poet and churchman John] Donne were among the first to recognize this dilemma. They were among the first to demand a merciful release from the new "technology" of their times.

The Eighteenth Century

Still, those men were essayists and philosophers. Fortunately, by the eighteenth century, a few members of the medical profession had begun speaking about their responsibility to the patient. They stressed the importance of a natural and humane way of dying. For instance, in his "Oratio de Euthanasia" of 1794, Paradys, a physician, recommended an "easy death" for a patient, especially one who is incurable and suffering. Like More and Donne, he saw medical progress as a sword that cut both ways, with the patient sometimes a victim.

Further, by this time, it was not just the physician who had views on life and death. One result of the Renaissance and the Reformation was a general humanitarian enlightenment. The common man was more informed. For example, he knew that suicide was no longer an unforgivable sin, and that civil and criminal law had softened toward the victim. . . .

For the eighteenth-century rationalists, then, it was ridiculous and presumptuous to inflate suicide, an intensely private act, into a monstrous crime. In 1777, a year after his death, the Scottish philosopher David Hume's essay "Of Suicide" was published. "When life has become a burden," he had written, "both courage and prudence should engage us to rid ourselves at once of existence." With this more informed attitude on the part of Hume and others, another phase had begun. A supportive attitude toward suicide surfaced publicly. For instance, Joseph Addison's play *Cato*, extolling the noblest Roman suicide of all, was greeted each night by thunderous applause from Whigs and Tories alike. In 1788, Horace Walpole commenting on the statutes and penalties imposed on suicides, referred to such practices as the "absurd stake and highway of our ancestors."

Similarly, in France—where suicide laws and penalties had once been equally stringent—there were references in [French philosopher Jean-Jacques] Rousseau to a "virtuous suicide" due to increased suffering and wastefulness. . . . By 1870, with a swing back to liberal and democratic ideals, the government eventually forbade discrimination against anyone—even suicides—in the matter of burial, and insisted on the application of proper honors, whether in religious or in civil funerals.

From the Nineteenth Century to 1940

In the early part of the nineteenth century, one Carl F.H. Marx presented an oral thesis, "Medical Euthanasia." In it he criticized physicians who treated diseases rather than the patient, and who, as a result, lost interest and abandoned the patient when they couldn't find a cure. Marx insisted that the physician "is not expected to have a remedy for death, but for the skillful alleviation of suffering, and he should know how to apply it when all hope has departed." Seveal years later, [German philosopher Arthur] Schopenhauer stressed man's "unassailable title to his own life and person. . . . It will be generally found that, as soon as the terrors of life reach the point at which they outweigh the terrors of death, a man will put an end to his life."

While Schopenhauer may have been speaking of a more general malaise as a basis for contemplating suicide, man's right to define the quality of his own life and death was an inalienable assertion of his will, whatever the reasons. (It was [Friedrich] Nietzsche who, only a few years later, spoke of the thought of suicide as "a strong consolation . . . one can get through many a bad night with it." Both physicians and philosophers were speaking about a person's right to decide for himself. Man was increasingly in charge of his environment. The Renaissance had rekindled many classical values, not the least of which was that a man was a free agent, provided he was acting rationally. . . .

In 1897, French sociologist Émile Durkheim published *Le Suicide*, which examined suicide as a social fact and analyzed it accordingly, somewhat demystifying the phenomenon. A few years later, the German psychiatrist/philosopher Alfred Hoche coined the term *Bilanz Selbstmord*—"balance-sheet suicide"—in citing examples of apparently rational suicide by those who had reviewed their lives, weighed the pros and cons, and decided, quite deliberately, that death was preferable to life. The concept of physical and mental pain, then, was considered by physicians and writers as a possible justification for ending one's life.

In fact, in both America and Europe over the next three decades, the subject of euthanasia was becoming less academic and more a matter of what *should* be done—not only by physicians but by the law and governing bodies. For instance, in England in 1901, Dr. C.E. Goddard addressed the Willesden and District Medical Society in northwest London. His speech, "Suggestions in Favor of Terminating Absolutely Hopeless Cases of Injury and Disease," made an appeal for legalizing euthanasia as a way to avoid suffering for terminal patients. Hopeless idiots, imbeciles, and "monstrosities" were included—"Those having no will power nor intelligence of their own, and being a burden to themselves, and especially their friends and society, [and] of course absolutely incapable of improvement." Goddard's speech was received with both interest and alarm.

Five years later, in the United States, a bill dealing with euthanasia was introduced in the Ohio legislature. An editor of the *Independent* wrote about the bill:

> When an adult of sound mind has been fatally hurt and is so ill that recovery is impossible or is suffering extreme physical pain without hope of relief, his physician, if not a relative and if not interested in any way in the person's estate, may ask his patient in the presence of three witnesses if he or she is ready to die. . . . Three other physicians are to be consulted.

The writer went on to say that although the bill was supported by some eminent people, civilization at that time was not ready to consider such legislation seriously. An article in the *Outlook* ("Shall We Legalize Homicide?") listed some dangers: Guardians and relatives could rid themselves too easily of "burdens," inept doctors could conceal their failures, inheritors would he tempted to stoop to corrupt practices and pressures, and confidence in doctors would be undermined. "It would add to the terror of the sickbed by stimulating fears. . . . The patient would look to the visit of the physician with dread." A *New York Times* editorial compared the practice of euthanasia to "practices of savages in all parts of the world." Not surprisingly, when the Ohio bill was sent to the Committee on Medical Jurisprudence, it was defeated by a vote of seventy-eight to twenty-two.

Still, the fact that the bill was proposed at all—and received almost 25 percent of the vote—indicated that people were concerned about controlling the manner of their dying.

One of the most important attempts to incorporate euthanasia into law took place in England in 1931. Dr. C. Killick Millard, health officer for the city of Leicester, gave his presidential address before the Society of Officers of Health. It was during this time that there had been a spate of scholarly articles and two books in support of euthanasia and its legalization. Perhaps Millard's speech was inevitable. Still, he startled his audience by devoting his entire talk ("A Plea for Legalization of Euthanasia") to an appeal for a change in the law. He quoted extensively from More's *Utopia* and spoke of the anguish of those who die lingering deaths, "by inches." In a subsequent article in *Fortnightly Review*, he presented his specific proposals in a draft bill entitled "The Voluntary Euthanasia Legalization Bill." It included the following provisions:

1. An application for a euthanasia permit may be filed by a dying person stating that he has been informed by two medical practitioners that he is suffering from a fatal and incurable disease, and that the process of death is likely to be protracted and painful.

2. The application must be attested by a magistrate and accompanied by two medical certificates.

3. The application and certificates must be examined by the patient and relatives interviewed by a "euthanasia referee."

4. A court will then review the application, certificates, the testimony of the referee and any other representatives of the patient. It will then issue a permit to receive euthanasia to the applicant and a permit to administer euthanasia to the medical practitioner (or euthanizer).

5. The permit would be valid for a specified period, within which the patient would determine if and when he wished to use it.

Millard added that the final responsibility might lie with either the physician or the patient—that a lethal dose could, in fact, be placed by the patient's bedside to be taken at his discretion. ("I am inclined myself to think," he wrote, "that the responsibility for the actual *coup de grace* should rest with the patient.")

Despite a mixed reaction to Millard's proposals, much support came from prominent people—(churchmen, academics, writers, aristocrats and other physicians). Eventually, in 1935, the British Voluntary Euthanasia Society was formed specifically to promote the bill drafted by Millard. . . .

Unfortunately for Millard and his colleagues, the bill had as many—if not more—opponents as supporters. In 1936 it was defeated in the House of Lords, after a heated discussion, by a vote of thirty-five to fourteen. The Euthanasia Society, however, continued to campaign for the rights of the terminally ill and for appropriate legislation (which was not considered in Parliament again until 1950). Millard continued as spokesman. After the bill was defeated, he said he believed that "the substitution of a quick and painless death in certain cases for a death which was slow and agonizing would be regarded hereafter as one of the great reforms of the age."

In 1937 in Nebraska, a bill modeled after its English predecessor was introduced in the state legislature by Senator John Comstock. Entitled the Voluntary Euthanasia Act, the bill was sponsored by Dr. Inez Philbrick, a former member of the University of Nebraska faculty. It was, however, referred to a committee, indefinitely postponed, and never acted upon.

Concern about the failure to enact legislation and admiration for the British model led to the founding in 1938 of the Euthanasia Society of America. Announcing the formation of the Society, Reverend Charles Francis Potter explained that members "subscribed to the belief that, with adequate safeguards, it should be made legal to allow incurable sufferers to choose immediate death rather than await it in agony.". . .

On January 26, 1939, a bill to legalize euthanasia in New York was proposed by the Society's treasurer, Charles Nixdorff. "Spurred by recent 'mercy killing' cases," the January 27 *New York Times* reported, "and by mounting inquiries from persons suffering from incurable diseases, the Euthanasia Society of America offered yesterday a proposed legislative bill which would legalize the putting to death of incurables in this State when the patient wants to die." Similar to the British bill, which concentrated on terminally ill adults, it was never introduced into the legislature and was shelved until after [World War II].

The First Euthanasia Society in the United States

CHARLES FRANCIS POTTER

*Charles Francis Potter was a Unitarian minister and a bibli-
cal scholar who became a central figure in the euthanasia
movement during the first half of the twentieth century. In this
selection he announces the establishment of the National Society for the Legalization of Euthanasia in 1938. He declares
that one of the aims of the society is to lobby to legalize euthanasia. Potter notes that more than fifty eminent figures
from the United States and Great Britain are on the board of
directors and the advisory board of the new organization. In
addition to promoting euthanasia, the Euthanasia Society advocated eugenics laws, promoting the mass sterilization of
prison inmates and the "mercy killing" of the mentally handicapped. After World War II, news of Hitler's euthanasia program in Germany, including the killing of deformed children,
the mentally ill, and the elderly, caused people to question
the morality of the Euthanasia Society. In the 1950s, the society's ideas were generally rejected. However, in the 1960s
and 1970s, when the civil rights movement promoted autonomy and self-determination, the American public started to
accept passive euthanasia, as an individual's right to refuse
livesaving medical treatment, paving the way for initiatives
in legislation. Potter and many of his colleagues in the euthanasia movement were also at the vanguard of campaigns*

Charles Francis Potter, announcement of the formation of The Euthanasia Society, New York, January 16, 1938.

*that promoted divorce, birth control, women's equality, and
the abolition of capital punishment. Potter wrote numerous
books, including* Creative Personality: The Next Step in Evo-
lution, The Faiths Men Live By, The Great Religious Leaders, *and* The Preacher and I.

A nnouncement was made Jan. 16, 1938, of the formation
in New York City of a National Society for the Legalization of Euthanasia, commonly known as "mercy-killing." The
group forming the Board of Directors and the Advisory
Board of the new society includes over fifty eminent American and British men and women with representatives from
the legal, medical, educational, ministerial, and literary professions. Members of the faculties of Harvard, Cornell, Ohio
State, California, Chicago, Smith, McGill, Duke, Vermont,
Wisconsin, Indiana, and Oxford Universities are included.

The purposes of the Society embrace not only the conducting of a national campaign of education on the subject
and the maintenance of a central headquarters for information and free literature, but also the preparation and introduction of bills into state legislatures and at Washington.

The establishing of the Euthanasia Society is in response
to a real need increasingly recognized by the thoughtful
people of this country. I have in my office letters from over
fifty eminent men and women of this country and England
enthusiastically accepting my invitation to serve on the Advisory Board of the Euthanasia Society. These letters afford
us a cross-section view of public sentiment. Only a few dec-
linations were received and most of these were due to the
fact that individuals did not want to expose to criticism the
institutions with which they are connected. . . .

Personally, my experiences as a clergyman for many
years have forced me to recognize the necessity for laws
permitting euthanasia in certain cases and under proper
restrictions. I have seen many middle-aged and elderly persons, mostly women, dying in prolonged agony from such

diseases as cancer. They have begged me to bring them secretly some quick-acting poison pills to put them out of their misery.

More than that, I have known of cases where whole families have been forced to endure the terrible mental anguish of watching the tortured breathing of loved ones for weeks before the last gasp. The mental effect upon relatives of sufferers is of incalculable harm.

Those opponents of euthanasia who claim that a sufferer is only a coward if he or she wishes to end his life, forget that most such sufferers are much more concerned about the anguish they are causing their dear ones than they are about their own pain.

I sense a growing demand on the part of thoughtful people everywhere that the ancient taboos should be lifted in order that the supreme mercy be no longer withheld from those who will certainly die within a few weeks or months but are kept alive only to suffer increasing anguish.

"Euthanasia" in Nazi Germany

U.S. HOLOCAUST MEMORIAL MUSEUM

The following article describes the Nazi "euthanasia" program that killed thousands of people in Germany and Austria during World War II. The Nazis used the term euthanasia *as a euphemism, as their purpose was not to relieve suffering but to kill people with mental and physical handicaps. The forerunner of the program was a sterilization campaign, begun in 1934, that aimed to produce a superior Aryan race by preventing people with so-called genetic defects (mental handicaps and schizophrenia in the majority of cases) from reproducing. An estimated three hundred thousand to four hundred thousand people were forcibly sterilized. In 1939 Hitler decreed a euthanasia program that targeted "patients considered incurable," which meant the physically and mentally handicapped. The group later included prisoners, including Jews, Gypsies, Russians, Poles, and Germans. From 1939 to 1945 more than two hundred thousand people were killed under the euthanasia program. In subsequent decades, opponents of euthanasia and assisted suicide have cited the example of Nazi Germany to bolster their claim that officially sanctioned mercy killing can be used to deplorable ends. This article is from the Web site of the U.S. Holocaust Memorial Museum, based in Washington, D.C.*

In October 1939, Hitler himself initiated a decree which empowered physicians to grant a "mercy death" to "patients considered incurable according to the best available human judgment of their state of health." The intent of the so-called "euthanasia" program, however, was not to relieve the suffering of the chronically ill. The Nazi regime used the term as a euphemism: its aim was to exterminate the mentally ill and the handicapped, thus "cleansing" the "Aryan" race of persons considered genetically defective and a financial burden to society.

The idea of killing the incurably ill was posed well before 1939. In the 1920s, debate on this issue centered on a book coauthored by Alfred Hoche, a noted psychiatrist, and Karl Binding, a prominent scholar of criminal law. They argued that economic savings justified the killing of "useless lives" ("idiots" and "congenitally crippled"). Economic deprivation during World War I provided the context for this idea. During the war, patients in asylums had ranked low on the list for rationing of food and medical supplies, and as a result, many died from starvation or disease. More generally, the war undermined the value attached to individual life and, combined with Germany's humiliating defeat, led many nationalists to consider ways to regenerate the nation as a whole at the expense of individual rights.

In 1935 Hitler stated privately that "in the event of war, [he] would take up the question of euthanasia and enforce it" because "such a problem would be more easily solved" during wartime. War would provide both a cover for killing and a pretext—hospital beds and medical personnel would be freed up for the war effort. The upheaval of war and the diminished value of human life during wartime would also, Hitler believed, mute expected opposition. To make the connection to the war explicit, Hitler's decree [issued in October 1939] was backdated to September 1, 1939, the day Germany invaded Poland.

Fearful of public reaction, the Nazi regime never proposed a formal "euthanasia" law. Unlike the forced sterilizations [that the regime began carrying out according to the "Sterilization Law" of 1934], the killing of patients in mental asylums and other institutions was carried out in secrecy. The code name was "Operation T4," a reference to Tiergartenstrasse 4, the address of the Berlin Chancellery offices where the program was headquartered.

Key Role of Physicians

Physicians, the most highly Nazified professional group in Germany, were key to the success of "T-4," since they organized and carried out nearly, all aspects of the operation. One of Hitler's personal physicians, Dr. Karl Brandt, headed the program, along with Hitler's Chancellery chief, Philip Bouhler. T-4 targeted adult patients in all government or church-run sanatoria and nursing homes. These institutions were instructed by the Interior Ministry to collect questionnaires about the state of health and capacity for work of all their patients, ostensibly as part of a statistical survey.

The completed forms were, in turn, sent to expert "assessors"—physicians, usually psychiatrists, who made up "review commissions." They marked each name with a "+" in red pencil, meaning death, or a "–" in blue pencil, meaning life, or "?" for cases needing additional assessment. These medical experts rarely examined any of the patients and made their decisions from the questionnaires alone. At every step, the medical authorities involved were usually expected to quickly process large numbers of forms.

The doomed were bused to killing centers in Germany and Austria. [These centers were] walled-in fortresses, mostly former psychiatric hospitals, castles, and a former prison—at Hartheim, Sonnenstein, Grafeneck, Bernburg, Hadamar, and Brandenburg. In the beginning, patients were killed by lethal injection. But by 1940, Hitler, on the advice of Dr. Werner Heyde, suggested that carbon monoxide gas be used as the preferred method of killing. Experimental gassings had first been carried out at Brandenburg Prison in 1939. There, gas chambers were disguised as showers complete with fake nozzles in order to deceive victims—prototypes of the killing centers' facilities built in occupied Poland later in the war.

Again, following procedures that would later be instituted in the extermination camps, workers removed the corpses from the chambers, extracted gold teeth, then burned large numbers of bodies together in crematoria. Urns filled with ashes were prepared in the event the family of the deceased requested the remains. Physicians using fake names prepared death certificates falsifying the cause of death, and sent letters of condolences to relatives.

Meticulous records discovered after the war documented 70,273 deaths by gassing at the six "euthanasia" centers between January 1940 and August 1941. (This total included up to 5,000 Jews; all Jewish mental patients were killed regardless of their ability to work or the seriousness of their illness.) A detailed report also recorded the estimated savings from the killing of institutionalized patients.

Protests from a Few Church Leaders

The secrecy surrounding the T-4 program broke down quickly. Some staff members were indiscreet while drinking in local pubs after work. Despite precautions, errors were made: hairpins turned up in urns sent to relatives of male victims; the cause of death was listed as appendicitis when the patient had the appendix removed years before. The town of Hadamar school pupils called the gray transport buses "killing crates" and threatened each other with the taunt, "You'll end up in the Hadamar ovens!" The thick smoke from the incinerator was said to be visible every day over Hadamar (where, in midsummer 1941, the staff celebrated the cremation of their 10,000th patient with beer and wine served in the crematorium).

A handful of church leaders, notably the Bishop of Münster, Clemens August Count von Galen, local judges, and parents of victims protested the killings. One judge, Lothar Kreyssig, instituted criminal proceedings against Bouhler for murder; Kreyssig was prematurely retired. A few physicians protested. Karl Bonhöffer, a leading psychiatrist, and his son Dietrich, a Protestant minister who actively opposed the regime, urged church groups to pressure church-run institutions not to release their patients to T-4 authorities.

In response to such pressures, Hitler ordered a halt to Operation T-4 on August 24, 1941. Gas chambers from some of the "euthanasia" killing centers were dismantled and shipped to extermination camps in occupied Poland. In late 1941 and 1942, they were rebuilt and used for the "final solution to the Jewish question." Similarly redeployed from T-4 were future extermination camp commandants Christian Wirth, Franz Stangl, Franz Reichleitner, the doctor Irmfried Eberl, as well as about 100 others—doctors, male nurses, and clerks, who applied their skills in Treblinka, Belzec, and Sobibor [extermination camps].

The "euthanasia" killings continued, however, under a different, decentralized form. Hitler's regime continued to send to physicians and the general public the message that mental patients were "useless eaters" and "life unworthy of life." In 1941, the film *Ich klage an* ("I accuse") in which a professor kills his incurably ill wife, was viewed by 18 million people. Doctors were encouraged to decide on their own who should live or die. Killing became part of hospital routine as infants, children, and adults were put to death by starvation, poisoning, and injections. Killings even continued in some of Germany's mental asylums, such as Kaufbeuren, weeks after Allied troops had occupied surrounding areas.

Killings in Concentration Camps

Between the middle of 1941 and the winter of 1944–45, in a program known under code "14f13," experienced psychiatrists from the T-4 operation were sent to concentration camps to weed out prisoners too ill to work. After superficial medical screenings, designated inmates, Jews, Gypsies, Russians, Poles, Germans, and others, were sent to those "euthanasia" centers where gas chambers still had not been dismantled, at Bernburg and Hartheim, where they were gassed. At least 20,000 people are believed to have died under the 14f13 program.

Outside of Germany, thousands of mental patients in the occupied territories of Poland, Russia, and East Prussia were also killed by the *Einsatzgruppen* squads (SS and special police units) that followed in the wake of the invading German army. Between September 29 and November 1, 1939, these units shot about 3,700 mental patients in asylums in the region of Bromberg, Poland. In December 1939 and January 1940, SS units gassed 1,558 patients from Polish asylums in specially adapted gas vans, in order to make room for military and SS barracks. Although regular army units did not officially participate in such "cleansing" actions as general policy, some instances of their involvement have been documented.

In all, between 200,000 and 250,000 mentally and physically handicapped persons were murdered from 1939 to 1945 under the T-4 and other "euthanasia" programs. The magnitude of these crimes and the extent to which they prefigured the "Final Solution" [the extermination of European Jews] continue to be studied. Further, in an age of genetic engineering and renewed controversy over mercy killings of the incurably ill, ethical and moral issues of concern to physicians, scientists, and lay persons alike remain vital.

The Euthanasia Debate in the 1950s and 1960s

IAN DOWBIGGIN

In the following selection, Ian Dowbiggin explains how the debate over euthanasia took a drastic turn in 1957 when Pope Pius XII spoke in favor of passive euthanasia. The head of the Catholic Church said that while the church opposed mercy killing, dying patients could refuse extraordinary medical treatment to extend their lives. During the same period, an Episcopalian minister made a much more radical argument. Joseph Fletcher introduced the theory of "situational ethics," which holds that there are no absolute moral standards that guide medical treatment. Instead, the individual circumstances of a patient's condition must be considered when deciding what course of action to take. Fletcher argued that patients have a right to choose euthanasia. However, other scholars disagreed with Fletcher for various reasons detailed in the selection. Dowbiggin is a professor of history at the University of Prince Edward Island in Canada. A scholar in the history of medicine, he is the author of A Merciful End: The Euthanasia Movement in Modern America, *from which the selection was taken.*

Few predicted it, but euthanasia suddenly burst onto the national scene in the 1960s and 1970s as an issue of sustained public interest. Under the shadow of nuclear war, in the wake of the thalidomide tragedy, amid a demoralizing war in southeast Asia, and in response to the aging of the U.S. population and the mounting use of life-prolonging medical technology, Americans became increasingly obsessed with death and terminal illness as experiences that deserved detailed study and discussion. As a national dialogue on dying spread, the idea of death with minimal pain and loss of individual dignity grew popular. Thanks to the rising public interest in the concepts of patient autonomy and individual rights, euthanasia ceased being interpreted as a predominantly social or biological matter and was largely transformed into a personal issue. Increasingly it was viewed as a civil liberty, a freedom *from* interference in one's personal life, rather than a legal practice monitored (and possibly applied) by the state. Privacy became the keyword of the new, revitalized euthanasia movement, and the term "euthanasia" was steadily replaced by the phrase "the right to die."

This change helped to break the stalemate reached by the 1950s when euthanasia was chiefly defined in terms of the deliberate killing of terminally ill patients, and when discussion of euthanasia was hopelessly polarized. Ironically and unexpectedly, impetus for change came from Pope Pius XII, who, in 1957, announced that passive euthanasia was permissible, that patients could refuse extraordinary treatment to prolong their lives without violating Christian teaching. In a single stroke, the Pope helped to alter the terrain beneath the entire debate over euthanasia, making a constructive dialogue possible among those concerned about medical care for the dying and ending the standoff between the ESA [Euthanasia Society of America] and its opponents in the 1940s and 1950s.

But with the disappearance of the familiar fault lines between euthanasia advocates and their opponents, the old unity of the euthanasia movement began to dissolve as various groups advanced their own interpretations of the right to die. Gone were the customary eugenic justifications for mercy killing and the proposals for state-run euthanasia programs. To many Americans, euthanasia came to mean the right to refuse treatment. However, social and economic justifications for euthanasia did not disappear—a symptom of the mixed signals emitted by the 1960s counterculture— nor did the illiberal and elitist tendencies, stretching back to the Progressive era [1920–1940], which historically have characterized the campaign to legalize euthanasia.

Yes to Passive, Voluntary Euthanasia

It was a pope, of all people, who truly revolutionized the national discussion over the right to die. On 24 February 1957 Pope Pius XII spoke to an international gathering of anesthesiologists and, while upholding traditional Catholic opposition to mercy killing, added that there was no reason that dying persons should endure unusual pain. Physicians, he stated, were permitted to use pain relievers even if they shortened a dying patient's life, though doctors should never administer pain-killing drugs against someone's will or with the intention of killing a patient. Christians were still encouraged to accept physical suffering as heroic imitation of Christ's passion on the Cross, but the Pope declared that dying patients were under no obligation to accept extraordinary medical treatment simply to extend their lives.

The Pope's announcement in favor of passive (not active) voluntary euthanasia caught euthanasia proponents off guard. Since the ESA's inception, its leadership had crafted its message to the American public in terms of legalizing voluntary, active euthanasia. Euthanasia advocates had tended to ignore the issue of withdrawal of medical treatment for consenting, dying adults. Well into the 1950s, the ESA still included a sizable number of eugenically inclined members who were more interested in medical mercy killing. While figures such as [ESA founder] Charles Potter and [ESA activist] Eleanor Dwight Jones did not ignore the personal and humane virtues of individual choice-in-dying, they usually conflated these considerations with factors such as the savings to taxpayers and the emotional relief for friends and relatives. They appeared almost oblivious to what after the 1960s would become the swelling popular demand for an individual's right to refuse unwanted medical treatment. Hamstrung by their simultaneous commitments to birth control, eugenics, and population control, they seemed unable to conceptualize the right to refuse treatment as a purely humane step toward meeting the personal needs of terminally ill Americans. Both the Pope's address and the cultural changes of the 1960s compelled them to rethink their entire way of viewing euthanasia.

From the Catholic perspective, the Pope's gesture was brilliant strategy. Pius had been briefed extensively by his close friend, New York City's Francis Cardinal Spellman, a warhorse in the Church's battles with the ESA and Protestants and Other Americans United for the Separation of Church and State (POAU). Spellman was politically astute and, although a stern moralist, on a few topics was refreshingly open to new ideas. He knew as much as anyone in the Church that the times and attitudes of Americans were changing, notably American Catholics whose misgivings about Church teaching on sex and contraception would be more evident in the 1960s. Spellman did not want to budge on sexual teachings, but on the ethics of palliative care he was more flexible. Life-sustaining medical technology was making bedside decision-making more and more complex. Simply continuing to advocate a total ban on all forms of euthanasia was bound to be viewed as obstructionist and likely to discredit the Church in the long run. Conceding the right to refuse futile medical treatment might checkmate the ESA-led movement in favor of active euthanasia by raising questions about whether the latter was even necessary. Such a strategy might pressure euthanasia proponents to put their campaign in favor of active euthanasia on hold, which is precisely what they did.

Situational Ethics and Patient Autonomy

In taking the advice of Cardinal Spellman, Pope Pius XII was also reacting to the first signs that philosophers and legal theorists were studying euthanasia. One of the weaknesses of the euthanasia movement up to the 1950s was that, while there had been polemics aplenty, no philosopher had attempted a systematic defense of euthanasia as an integral part of an overall revision of medical ethics. Charles Potter had been defending euthanasia since the 1930s, but like his colleagues in the movement, he had written little that could serve as a sophisticated philosophical justification of mercy killing.

When Potter died in 1962, theologian Joseph Fletcher assumed Potter's unofficial title as the chief philosopher of the euthanasia movement. By then, Fletcher's 1954 book *Morals and Medicine* had become a best seller and had almost single-handedly launched the discipline of biomedical ethics, ending the dominance practicing physicians had exercised for years over bedside decision-making in medicine. Fletcher introduced the highly influential theory of "situational ethics," which stated that there were no absolute moral standards that guided medical treatment. The solution to any health-related dilemma depended solely on the particular circumstances surrounding a patient's condition. The wide readership of *Morals and Medicine* and Fletcher's other books testified to the success he enjoyed between the 1950s and his death in 1991 breaking down barriers to the acceptance of euthanasia.

Fletcher, born in 1905 in Newark, New Jersey, ranks with Potter, Jones, [1990s physician-assisted suicide crusader] Jack Kevorkian, and [euthanasia advocate] Hemlock Society co-founder Derek Humphry as the people who did the most for the right-to-die movement in twentieth-century America. Although he wrote on a variety of biomedical issues, Fletcher was most interested in euthanasia, devoting the bulk of his last thirty years to the cause. Like so many others in the movement, Fletcher supported euthanasia—what he often called "death control"—because he saw it as a kindred cause to birth control and reproductive rights for women. "Death control, like birth control," he stated, "is a matter of human dignity. Without it persons become puppets."

Fletcher fashioned a new rationale for euthanasia based primarily on the notion of patient autonomy. Fletcher's emphasis on what he called "the *personal* dimensions of morality in medical care" helped to forge a new alliance in the 1960s and 1970s between supporters of euthanasia and those who supported women's right to abortion.

An Episcopal minister, Fletcher in 1936 began pastoral counseling of patients in homes and hospitals while teaching Christian ethics at the Episcopal Theological School in Cambridge, Massachusetts. It was his clinical experience dealing with the terminally ill that stimulated his interest in euthanasia, but from the beginning Fletcher was temperamentally and intellectually disposed to embrace iconoclastic causes that stressed emancipation from traditional values. His involvement in organizations such as the American Birth Control League and the American Civil Liberties Union (ACLU) reflected this tendency. Long before the family planning movement began discussing a woman's right to terminate a pregnancy, Fletcher was defending abortion. Twice beaten unconscious while lecturing in the South for the Southern Tenants Farmers' Union, he became a member of the Soviet-American Friendship Society and the World Peace Council alter World War II, drawing the ire of Senator Joseph McCarthy, who called Fletcher "the Red Churchman." These experiences made him a natural ally of the ESA in its battles with the Roman Catholic Church in the forties and fifties. In 1959 he denounced the "authoritarianism" of Catholicism as "alien to our American life and thought where cultural and religious pluralism is the most vital principle." In fact, in the early 1940s, well before he became a target of McCarthyism, Fletcher and his friend [birth control advocate] Margaret Sanger had joined the ESA.

In *Morals and Medicine*, Fletcher rehearsed some of Potter's old justifications for euthanasia. Why did society not accept euthanasia when it accepted war and capital punishment as excusable types of killing? Fletcher asked. Similarly, he interpreted the Sixth Commandment to mean "thou shalt do no murder," rather than "thou shalt not kill." As an ethicist, he rejected "naturalism" as a rationale for euthanasia and instead stressed freedom to choose for people whose "integrity [was] threatened by disintegration.". . .

Involuntary Sterilization

Fletcher's spirited defense of eugenic sterilization in *Morals and Medicine* also cast a shadow over his insistence that he sought only "private choice" in euthanasia. In 1962 Fletcher became president of the Human Betterment Association of America (HBAA), the new name chosen in 1950 for Marian Olden's Birthright, Inc., which endorsed voluntary sterilization (vasectomy or tubal ligation, but not castration) as both a family planning and population control technique. Like so many members of the HBAA, Fletcher also recommended involuntary sterilization as a means of curbing the fertility of the mentally handicapped. As he declared in 1954, the "unborn" enjoyed a "complete *birthright* of a sound mind in a sound body," and this justified compulsory sterilization. "The interest of the public welfare" and the very "spiritual nature" of the individual permitted it. Even punitive sterilization of criminals was "ethically sound," according to Fletcher.

Such reasoning undermined Fletcher's claim to defend only voluntary euthanasia. If the mentally handicapped and criminals should be forced to undergo sterilization for social reasons, then why should the state stop short of ordering the mercy killing of severely disabled individuals? If their hospitalization and medical treatment entailed high costs to the community, if their quality of life appeared miserable in institutions, what prevented governments from taking measures to cut these costs in the name of "social justice" or "humanity"? Fletcher never answered these questions in *Morals and Medicine*. By stressing that there was no rational or Christian reason to regard life as sacred, that painful dying or disability caused the personality to disintegrate, and that it was "indecent to go on living" under certain circumstances, Fletcher's ethical philosophy was something less than a denunciation of involuntary euthanasia. This became clearer in 1977 when he argued that "mercy killing" was justified for "an incorrigible 'human vegetable,' whether spontaneously functioning or artificially supported, [who] is progressively degraded while constantly eating up private or public financial resources in violation of the distributive justice owed to others." "The needs of others have a stronger claim upon us morally" than those of such a patient, he concluded. Little wonder that critics charged that his support for elective euthanasia was merely a tactic designed to acclimatize public opinion to the idea of mercy killing without consent.

In later years, Fletcher would continue to play a prominent role in the right-to-die campaign, but in the meantime his *Morals and Medicine* sparked a lively debate. Few agreed with Fletcher, one exception being philosopher and ESA member Horace Kallen, who echoed Fletcher's point that elective euthanasia was not murder. . . .

Personal Liberty

The most important issue to emerge from the legal reaction to Fletcher's book was his affirmation of patient autonomy: that is, the right of patients to know the truth and their freedom to act on it as they saw fit. And the chief proponent of this viewpoint was the British legal scholar Glanville Williams.

Williams, like Fletcher, was hardly an impartial observer when it came to euthanasia. A member of both the ESA and the British Voluntary Euthanasia Legislation Society (VELS), Williams was already a convert to the cause when his *The Sanctity of Life and the Criminal Law* was published in 1957. Williams essentially repeated the argument made by anti-Catholic euthanasia advocates in the 1940s that the prohibition against euthanasia was defensible only on religious grounds and therefore did not apply to those who did not share such beliefs. To Williams, the main issue was "personal liberty." Relying heavily on Fletcher, Williams repeated the standard reasons for rethinking euthanasia: that the Sixth Commandment really meant "thou shalt do no murder," not "thou shalt not kill"; that a merciful "assisted suicide" with the patient's consent was permissible if killing in war or the execution of criminals was allowed; and that denying suffering human beings the right to die was denying them the love and compassion Christians owed one another. People were "entitled to demand the release of death from hopeless and helpless pain," and physicians ought to be immune to prosecution if they helped willing individuals to die. . . .

However, again like Fletcher, Williams waffled on the subject of restricting euthanasia to consenting, dying adults. Besides granting that euthanasia could be legalized in cases of "incapacitating but non-painful affliction, such as paralysis," he also broached the topic of involuntary euthanasia in cases of senile dementia and "hopelessly defective infants.". . .

The Ghost of Nazi Germany

Williams's theory that euthanasia could be condemned only for religious reasons was attacked by Yale Kamisar, a University of Minnesota Law School professor, on the grounds that there were legitimate nonreligious objections to euthanasia. Kamisar's criticism of Williams is as powerful today as it was in the 1950s. Euthanasia was unnecessary because doctors were getting better and better at controlling pain with medication. It was dangerous because physicians might misdiagnose an illness and thereby sway personal decisions to request euthanasia.

If suffering individuals were intent on suicide, it was better, he concluded, to take a "laissez-faire" attitude to the whole issue than pursue the enactment of a law "sanctioned by the state." Changing the law would be worse than leaving the law as it was.

Kamisar subscribed to the "wedge" argument used by Catholics and other religious opponents of euthanasia, contending that the "legal machinery initially designed to kill those who are a nuisance to themselves may someday engulf those who are a nuisance to others." Kamisar quoted at length from both ESA and VELS literature, which showed clear approval of involuntary as well as voluntary euthanasia. He also cited the Viennese-born psychiatrist Leo Alexander, who, after serving as consultant to the U.S. Office of the Chief Counsel for War Crimes at the Nuremberg Trials (1946–1947), argued that the horrors of the Holocaust could be traced to "small beginnings" before the Nazis took power in Germany. Once individuals such as [German psychiatrist] Karl Binding and "German criminal law scholar" Alfred Hoche [who together wrote the influential book *The Destruction of Life Devoid of Value*], started talking about lives "not worty to be lived," it became permissible to refer to some people being "better off dead." Given the tiny size and strength of America's euthanasia movement in the 1950s, Kamisar admitted that it was unlikely that Nazi-like atrocities would happen in America, but the internment of Japanese-Americans during the Second World War showed "*it can happen here unless we darn well make sure that it does not* by adamantly holding the line, by swiftly snuffing out what are or might be small beginnings of what we do not want to happen here."

Thus, by the end of the 1950s the arguments of people such as Kamisar, who linked euthanasia to the horrors of the Third Reich, put the euthanasia movement squarely on the defensive. The fact that Fletcher and Williams linked acceptance of euthanasia to approval of other such highly controversial policies as abortion and eugenic sterilization made their task of trying to win public opinion even more challenging. Juries might be sympathetic toward parents who ended the lives of their handicapped children, but that did not translate into any groundswell of opinion in favor of changing the laws regarding mercy killing.

The campaign for euthanasia was going so poorly by the early 1960s that even Joseph Fletcher recognized the need for a change of tactics. No one was better able to sniff the prevailing winds than Fletcher, and so he began to modify his approach to the issue in the short term, emphasizing the need to legalize passive euthanasia. He even proposed dropping the word "euthanasia" with its Nazi overtones, and replacing it with "dysthanasia," meaning "mercifully refusing to prolong the process of dying." "Dysthanasia" never caught on, but it is a measure of the demoralization sweeping the euthanasia movement at the time that militants such as Fletcher were so willing to soften their message in the struggle to win the backing of Americans. In the 1970s Fletcher and other radicals would recover their confidence and start campaigning for active euthanasia, but his moderation in the 1960s was a signal that the battle over the legalization of euthanasia was not going well for his side.

THE
HISTORY
OF
ISSUES

CHAPTER 2

Legal Battles

Chapter Preface

In 1986 the California-based Hemlock Society drafted a law that would legalize physician-assisted suicide and voluntary euthanasia. The proposed legislation generated much public discussion and debate.

Efforts of the Hemlock Society were bolstered by the 1990 *Cruzan* case, in which the U.S. Supreme Court established the legality of terminating medical treatment for an incurably ill patient. The Court's decision inspired advocates to aggressively promote the legalization of physician-assisted suicide. The Hemlock Society introduced its draft law as a ballot initiative in Washington in 1991, and in California in 1992. However, both attempts failed.

In promoting physician-assisted suicide, the Hemlock Society and its supporters asserted that individuals should not only have the right to choose the time of their death, as was established in *Cruzan*, but that they should have equal access to methods of causing death. This means that an incurably ill person has the right to request a physician's assistance in obtaining a lethal dose of medication.

Arguments in favor of physician-assisted suicide were further advanced by the organization Compassion in Dying in a 1994 court case contesting Washington's and New York's prohibition of physician-assisted suicide. The organization contended that the prohibition violated the equal protection provision of the Constitution. When the cases reached the federal courts, Washington's Ninth Circuit Court and New York's Second Circuit Court ruled against the ban. However, in 1997 the Supreme Court reversed the earlier courts' decisions and upheld the prohibition in the two states.

Also in 1994, right-to-die groups renewed their attempts

to legalize physician-assisted suicide, this time initiating legislation in Oregon. Oregon voters approved the proposed law, called the Death with Dignity Act, making the state the first in the United States to legalize assisted suicide. After facing several court challenges, the law finally took effect in October 1997.

The law, however, continued to meet stubborn resistance from opponents who had turned to the federal government for intervention. Right after the final Oregon vote in October, the federal Drug Enforcement Administration (DEA) declared that doctors prescribing controlled substances to help people kill themselves violated the 1971 Controlled Substances Act. The DEA was overruled in June 1998 when U.S. attorney general Janet Reno declared that doctors who followed Oregon's law would not be liable for federal prosecution.

Reno's ruling, however, did not end Oregon's legal woes. In 2001 the new U.S. attorney general, John Ashcroft, issued a directive stating that doctors who administer lethal injections with the intent of ending a patient's life would be prosecuted, risking loss of license and imprisonment.

In April 2002 a federal judge ruled that the Justice Department does not have the authority to overturn Oregon's law, adding that Ashcroft had attempted to "stifle an ongoing, earnest and profound debate in the various states concerning physician-assisted suicide." The issue may reach the U.S. Supreme Court. If it does, the high court's ruling will help determine the fate of efforts to legalize physician-assisted suicide.

The Quinlan Case Establishes the Right to Have Life Support Withdrawn

CHARLES E. HUGHES

In 1975 Karen Ann Quinlan lapsed into an irreversible coma after taking drugs and alcohol. Realizing Quinlan was in a deteriorating vegetative state, her parents asked the doctors to remove the respirator that kept her alive. When the doctors refused to do so, Joseph Quinlan, Karen's father, took the case to court. In 1976 the Supreme Court of New Jersey ultimately allowed Quinlan's father to remove her respirator, citing the constitutional right to privacy. After being removed from the respirator, Quinlan was transferred to a nursing home where she lived for ten more years without ever regaining consciousness. The Quinlan *case was important because it established the individual's right to forgo life-sustaining medical treatment. It also raised the importance of a patient's advance instructions on forgoing treatment and eventually led states to enact laws on such directives. The following selection is an excerpt from the New Jersey Supreme Court ruling in Quinlan's case. The opinion was written by Charles E. Hughes, the chief justice of the court.*

The central figure in this tragic case is Karen Ann Quinlan, a New Jersey resident. At the age of 22, she lies in a

---

Charles E. Hughes, *In the Matter of Karen Quinlan, an Alleged Incompetent,* Supreme Court of New Jersey, 1976.

debilitated and allegedly moribund state at Saint Clare's Hospital in Denville, New Jersey. The litigation has to do, in final analysis, with her life,—its continuance or cessation,—and the responsibilities, rights and duties, with regard to any fateful decision concerning it, of her family, her guardian, her doctors, the hospital, the State through its law enforcement authorities, and finally the courts of justice. . . .

Due to extensive physical damage fully described in the able opinion of the trial judge, Judge Muir, supporting that judgment, Karen allegedly was incompetent. Joseph Quinlan sought the adjudication of that incompetency. He wished to be appointed guardian of the person and property of his daughter. It was proposed by him that such letters of guardianship, if granted, should contain an express power to him as guardian to authorize the discontinuance of all extraordinary medical procedures now allegedly sustaining Karen's vital processes and hence her life, since these measures, he asserted, present no hope of her eventual recovery. A guardian ad litem was appointed by Judge Muir to represent the interest of the alleged incompetent. . . .

Karen's Medical Condition

On the night of April 15, 1975, for reasons still unclear, Karen Quinlan ceased breathing for at least two 15 minute periods. She received some ineffectual mouth-to-mouth resuscitation from friends. She was taken by ambulance to Newton Memorial Hospital. There she had a temperature of 100 degrees, her pupils were unreactive and she was unresponsive even to deep pain. The history at the time of her admission to that hospital was essentially incomplete and uninformative.

Three days later, Dr. Morse examined Karen at the request of the Newton admitting physician, Dr. McGee. He found her comatose with evidence of decortication, a condition relating to derangement of the cortex of the brain causing a physical posture in which the upper extremities are flexed and the lower extremities are extended. She required a respirator to assist her breathing. Dr. Morse was unable to obtain an adequate account of the circumstances and events leading up to Karen's admission to the Newton Hospital. Such initial history or etiology is crucial in neurological diagnosis. Relying as he did upon the Newton Memorial records and his own examination, he concluded that prolonged lack of oxygen in the bloodstream, anoxia, was identified with her condition as he saw it upon first observation. When she was later transferred to Saint Clare's Hospital she was still unconscious, still on a respirator and a tracheotomy had been performed. On her arrival Dr. Morse conducted extensive and detailed examinations. An electroencephalogram (EEG) measuring electrical rhythm of the brain was performed and Dr. Morse characterized the result as "abnormal but it showed some activity and was consistent with her clinical state." Other significant neurological tests, including a brain scan, an angiogram, and a lumbar puncture were normal in result. Dr. Morse testified that Karen has been in a state of coma, lack of consciousness, since he began treating her. He explained that there are basically two types of coma, sleep-like unresponsiveness and awake unresponsiveness. Karen was originally in a sleep-like unresponsive condition but soon developed "sleep-wake" cycles, apparently a normal improvement for comatose patients occurring within three to four weeks. In the awake cycle she blinks, cries out and does things of that sort but is still totally unaware of anyone or anything around her.

Dr. Morse and other expert physicians who examined her characterized Karen as being in a "chronic persistent vegetative state." Dr. Fred Plum, one of such expert witnesses, defined this as a "subject who remains with the capacity to maintain the vegetative parts of neurological function but who no longer has any cognitive function.". . .

It seemed to be the consensus not only of the treating physicians but also of the several qualified experts who testified in the case, that removal from the respirator would not conform to medical practices, standards and traditions.

The further medical consensus was that Karen in addition to being comatose is in a chronic and persistent "vegetative" state, having no awareness of anything or anyone around her and existing at a primitive reflex level. Although she does have some brain stem function (ineffective for respiration) and has other reactions one normally associates with being alive, such as moving, reacting to light, sound and noxious stimuli, blinking her eyes, and the like, the quality of her feeling impulses is unknown. She grimaces, makes sterotyped cries and sounds and has chewing motions. Her blood pressure is normal. . . .

Karen is described as emaciated, having suffered a weight loss of at least 40 pounds, and undergoing a continuing deteriorative process. Her posture is described as fetal-like and grotesque; there is extreme flexion-rigidity of the arms, legs and related muscles and her joints are severely rigid and deformed.

From all of this evidence, and including the whole testimonial record, several basic findings in the physical area are mandated. Severe brain and associated damage, albeit of uncertain etiology, has left Karen in a chronic and persistent vegetative state. No form of treatment which can cure or improve that condition is known or available. As nearly as may be determined, considering the guarded area of remote uncertainties characteristic of most medical science predictions, she can never be restored to cognitive or sapient life. Even with regard to the vegetative level and improvement therein (if such it may be called) the prognosis is extremely poor and the extent unknown if it should in fact occur.

She is debilitated and moribund and although fairly stable at the time of argument before us (no new information having been filed in the meanwhile in expansion of the record), no physician risked the opinion that she could live more than a year and indeed she may die much earlier. Excellent medical and nursing care so far has been able to ward off the constant threat of infection, to which she is peculiarly susceptible because of the respirator, the tracheal tube and other incidents of care in her vulnerable condition. Her life accordingly is sustained by the respirator and tubal feeding, and removal from the respirator would cause her death soon, although the time cannot be stated with more precision. . . .

Constitutional and Legal Issues

It is from this factual base that the Court confronts and responds to three basic issues:

1. Was the trial court correct in denying the specific relief requested by plaintiff [Joseph Quinlan], i.e., authorization for termination of the life-supporting apparatus, on the case presented to him? Our determination on that question is in the affirmative.

2. Was the court correct in withholding letters of guardianship from the plaintiff and appointing in his stead a stranger? On that issue our determination is in the negative.

3. Should this Court, in the light of the foregoing conclusions, grant declaratory relief to the plaintiff? On that question our Court's determination is in the affirmative.

This brings us to a consideration of the constitutional and legal issues underlying the foregoing determinations. . . .

It is the issue of the constitutional right of privacy that has given us most concern, in the exceptional circumstances of this case. Here a loving parent, qua parent and raising the rights of his incompetent and profoundly damaged daughter, probably irreversibly doomed to no more than a biologically vegetative remnant of life, is before the court. He seeks authorization to abandon specialized technological procedures which can only maintain for a time a body having no potential for resumption or continuance of other than a "vegetative" existence.

We have no doubt, in these unhappy circumstances, that if Karen were herself miraculously lucid for an interval (not altering the existing prognosis of the condition to which she would soon return) and perceptive of her irreversible condition, she could effectively decide upon discontinuance of the life-support apparatus, even if it meant the prospect of natural death. . . .

We have no hesitancy in deciding, in the instant diametrically opposite case, that no external compelling interest of the State could compel Karen to endure the unendurable, only to vegetate a few measurable months with no realistic possibility of returning to any semblance of cognitive or sapient life. We perceive no thread of logic distinguishing between such a choice on Karen's part and a similar choice which, under the evidence in this case, could be made by a competent patient terminally ill, riddled by cancer and suffering great pain; such a patient would not be resuscitated or put on a respirator . . . and a fortiori would not be kept against his will on a respirator.

Although the Constitution does not explicitly mention a right of privacy, Supreme Court decisions have recognized that a right of personal privacy exists and that certain areas of privacy are guaranteed under the Constitution. The Court has interdicted judicial intrusion into many aspects of personal decision, sometimes basing this restraint upon the conception of a limitation of judicial interest and responsibility, such as with regard to contraception and its relationship to family life and decision.

The Court in [the case of *Griswold v. Connecticut* (1965)] found the unwritten constitutional right of privacy to exist in the penumbra of specific guarantees of the Bill of Rights "formed by emanations from those guarantees that help give them life and substance." Presumably this right is broad enough to encompass a patient's decision to decline medical treatment under certain circumstances, in much the same way as it is broad enough to encompass a woman's decision to terminate pregnancy under certain conditions. . . .

The claimed interests of the State in this case are essentially the preservation and sanctity of human life and defense of the right of the physician to administer medical treatment according to his best judgment. In this case the doctors say that removing Karen from the respirator will conflict with their professional judgment. The plaintiff answers that Karen's present treatment serves only a maintenance function; that the respirator cannot cure or improve her condition but at best can only prolong her inevitable slow deterioration and death; and that the interests of the patient, as seen by her surrogate, the guardian, must be evaluated by the court as predominant, even in the face of an opinion contra by the present attending physicians. Plaintiff's distinction is significant. The nature of Karen's care and the realistic chances of her recovery are quite unlike those of the patients discussed in many of the cases where treatments were ordered. In many of those cases the medical procedure required (usually a transfusion) constituted a minimal bodily invasion and the chances of recovery and return to functioning life were very good. We think that the State's interest contra weakens and the individual's right to privacy grows as the degree of bodily invasion increases and the prognosis dims. Ultimately there comes a point at which the individual's rights overcome the State interest. It is for that reason that we believe Karen's choice, if she were competent to make it, would be vindicated by the law. Her prognosis is extremely poor,—she will never resume cognitive life. And the bodily invasion is very great,—she requires 24 hour intensive nursing care, antibiotics, the assistance of a respirator, a catheter and feeding tube.

Our affirmation of Karen's independent right of choice, however, would ordinarily be based upon her competency to assert it. The sad truth, however, is that she is grossly incompetent and we cannot discern her supposed choice based on the testimony of her previous conversations with friends, where such testimony is without sufficient probative weight. Nevertheless we have concluded that Karen's right of privacy may be asserted on her behalf by her guardian under the peculiar circumstances here present.

Karen's Family Will Act on Her Behalf

If a putative decision by Karen to permit this non-cognitive, vegetative existence to terminate by natural forces is regarded as a valuable incident of her right of privacy, as we believe it to be, then it should not be discarded solely on the basis that her condition prevents her conscious exercise of the choice. The only practical way to prevent destruction of the right is to permit the guardian and family of Karen to render their best judgment, subject to the qualifications hereinafter stated, as to whether she would exercise it in these circumstances. If their conclusion is in the affirmative this decision should be accepted by a society the overwhelming majority of whose members would, we think, in similar circumstances, exercise such a choice in the same way for themselves or for those closest to them. It is for this reason that we determine that Karen's right of privacy may be asserted in her behalf, in this respect, by her guardian and family under the particular circumstances presented by this record.

Regarding Mr. Quinlan's right of privacy, we agree with Judge Muir's conclusion that there is no parental constitutional right that would entitle him to a grant of relief in propria persona [in one's own person]. Insofar as a parental right of privacy has been recognized, it has been in the context of determining the rearing of infants and, as Judge Muir put it, involved "continuing life styles." Karen Quinlan is a 22 year old adult. Her right of privacy in respect of the matter before the Court is to be vindicated by Mr. Quinlan as guardian, as hereinabove determined.

The Medical Factor

Having declared the substantive legal basis upon which plaintiff's rights as representative of Karen must be deemed predicated, we face and respond to the assertion on behalf of defendants that our premise unwarrantably offends prevailing medical standards. We thus turn to consideration of the medical decision supporting the determination made below, conscious of the paucity of preexisting legislative and judicial guidance as to the rights and liabilities therein involved. . . .

Physicians distinguish between curing the ill and comforting and easing the dying; that they refuse to treat the curable as if they were dying or ought to die, and that they have sometimes refused to treat the hopeless and dying as if they were curable. In this sense. . . . many of them have refused to inflict an undesired prolongation of the process of dying on a patient in irreversible condition when it is clear that such "therapy" offers neither human nor humane benefit. We think these attitudes represent a balanced implementation of a profoundly realistic perspective on the meaning of life and death and that they respect the whole Judeo-Christian tradition of regard for human life. No less would they seem consistent with the moral matrix of medicine, "to heal," very much in the sense of the endless mission of the law, "to do justice."

Yet this balance, we feel, is particularly difficult to perceive and apply in the context of the development by advanced technology of sophisticated and artificial life-sustaining devices. For those possibly curable, such devices are of great value, and, as ordinary medical procedures, are essential. Consequently . . . they are necessary because of the ethic of medical practice. But in light of the situation in the present case (while the record here is somewhat hazy in distinguishing between "ordinary" and "extraordinary" measures), one would have to think that the use of the same respirator or like support could be considered "ordinary" in the context of the possibly curable patient but "extraordinary" in the context of the forced sustaining by cardio-respiratory processes of an irreversibly doomed patient. . . .

The evidence in this case convinces us that the focal point of decision should be the prognosis as to the reasonable possibility of return to cognitive and sapient life, as distinguished from the forced continuance of that biological vegetative existence to which Karen seems to be doomed.

In summary of the present Point of this opinion, we conclude that the state of the pertinent medical standards and practices which guided the attending physicians in this matter is not such as would justify this Court in deeming itself bound or controlled thereby in responding to the case for declaratory relief established by the parties on the record before us. . . .

The Court Rules

We herewith declare the following affirmative relief on behalf of the plaintiff. Upon the concurrence of the guardian and family of Karen, should the responsible attending physicians conclude that there is no reasonable possibility of Karen's ever emerging from her present comatose condition to a cognitive, sapient state and that the life-support apparatus now being administered to Karen should be discontinued, they shall consult with the hospital "Ethics Committee" or like body of the institution in which Karen is then hospitalized. If that consultative body agrees that there is no reasonable possibility of Karen's ever emerging from her present comatose condition to a cognitive, sapient state, the present life-support system may be withdrawn and said action shall be without any civil or criminal liability therefor on the part of any participant, whether guardian, physician, hospital or others. We herewith specifically so hold.

The Law Requires Clear Evidence of a Patient's Wish to Forgo Life-Sustaining Treatment

WILLIAM REHNQUIST

In January 1983 Nancy Cruzan was in a car accident that severely damaged her brain, causing her to deteriorate into a vegetative state. She could breathe on her own, but could take in food and water only through a feeding tube. Cruzan's parents, knowing their daughter was practically dead, asked the doctors to remove the tube to let her die. They refused, and the Cruzans had to go to court. In 1988 a Missouri probate court allowed the Cruzans to remove the feeding tube. However, the Missouri Supreme Court later reversed the lower court's decision, stating that there was no "clear and convincing evidence" of Nancy's wishes, which Missouri law requires. The Cruzans appealed to the U.S. Supreme Court. In this selection, Chief Justice William Rehnquist presents the majority opinion, upholding the ruling of the Missouri Supreme Court. The U.S. Supreme Court had previously recognized the constitutional right of a competent person (one able to communicate his or her wishes) to decline treatment. The Cruzan *case determined that there must be clear evidence of a pa-*

William Rehnquist, majority opinion, *Cruzan v. Director, Missouri Department of Health*, U.S. Supreme Court, 1990.

tient's wishes to refuse medical treatment in order for the Court to allow passive euthanasia for an individual. The case led to the passage of the Patient Self-Determination Act in 1990, which required all health care institutions receiving federal funds to tell patients about their right to fill out advance directives (statements indicating their wishes for treatment should they become incompetent) and to refuse medical care. Rehnquist was appointed chief justice by President Ronald Reagan in 1986.

Petitioner Nancy Beth Cruzan was rendered incompetent as a result of severe injuries sustained during an automobile accident. Copetitioners Lester and Joyce Cruzan, Nancy's parents and coguardians, sought a court order directing the withdrawal of their daughter's artificial feeding and hydration equipment after it became apparent that she had virtually no chance of recovering her cognitive faculties. The Supreme Court of Missouri held that, because there was no clear and convincing evidence of Nancy's desire to have life-sustaining treatment withdrawn under such circumstances, her parents lacked authority to effectuate such a request. We granted certiorari [agreed to hear oral arguments and to issue an opinion] and now affirm.

On the night of January 11, 1983, Nancy Cruzan lost control of her car as she traveled down Elm Road in Jasper County, Missouri. The vehicle overturned, and Cruzan was discovered lying face down in a ditch without detectable respiratory or cardiac function. Paramedics were able to restore her breathing and heartbeat at the accident site, and she was transported to a hospital in an unconscious state. An attending neurosurgeon diagnosed her as having sustained probable cerebral contusions compounded by significant anoxia (lack of oxygen). The Missouri trial court in this case found that permanent brain damage generally results after 6 minutes in an anoxic state; it was estimated that Cruzan was deprived of oxygen from 12 to 14 minutes.

She remained in a coma for approximately three weeks, and then progressed to an unconscious state in which she was able to orally ingest some nutrition. In order to ease feeding and further the recovery, surgeons implanted a gastrostomy feeding and hydration tube in Cruzan with the consent of her then husband. Subsequent rehabilitative efforts proved unavailing. She now lies in a Missouri state hospital in what is commonly referred to as a persistent vegetative state: generally, a condition in which a person exhibits motor reflexes but evinces no indications of significant cognitive function. The State of Missouri is bearing the cost of her care.

After it had become apparent that Nancy Cruzan had virtually no chance of regaining her mental faculties, her parents asked hospital employees to terminate the artificial nutrition and hydration procedures. All agree that such a removal would cause her death. The employees refused to honor the request without court approval. The parents then sought and received authorization from the state trial court for termination. The court found that a person in Nancy's condition had a fundamental right under the State and Federal Constitution to refuse or direct the withdrawal of "death prolonging procedures." The court also found that Nancy's expressed thoughts at age twenty-five in somewhat serious conversation with a housemate friend that, if sick or injured, she would not wish to continue her life unless she could live at least halfway normally suggests that, given her present condition, she would not wish to continue on with her nutrition and hydration.

Missouri Supreme Court Rejected Parents' Request

The Supreme Court of Missouri reversed by a divided vote. The court recognized a right to refuse treatment embodied in the common law doctrine of informed consent, but expressed skepticism about the application of that doctrine in the circumstances of this case, *Cruzan v. Harmon*. The court also declined to read a broad right of privacy into the State Constitution which would "support the right of a person to refuse medical treatment in every circumstance," and expressed doubt as to whether such a right existed under the United States Constitution. It then decided that the Missouri Living Will statute (1986), embodied a state policy strongly favoring the preservation of life. The court found that Cruzan's statements to her roommate regarding her desire to live or die under certain conditions were "unreliable for the purpose of determining her intent," "and thus insufficient to support the coguardians' claim to exercise substituted judgment on Nancy's behalf." It rejected the argument that Cruzan's parents were entitled to order the termination of her medical treatment, concluding that no person can assume that choice for an incompetent in the absence of the formalities required under Missouri's Living Will statutes or the clear and convincing inherently reliable evidence absent here.

The court also expressed its view that "[b]road policy questions bearing on life and death are more properly addressed by representative assemblies" than judicial bodies.

We granted certiorari to consider the question of whether Cruzan has a right under the United States Constitution which would require the hospital to withdraw life-sustaining treatment from her under these circumstances.

At common law, even the touching of one person by another without consent and without legal justification was a battery. Before the turn of the century [1891], this Court observed that "[n]o right is held more sacred, or is more carefully guarded by the common law, than the right of every individual to the possession and control of his own person, free from all restraint or interference of others, unless by clear and unquestionable authority of law" (*Union Pacific R. Co. v. Botsford*). This notion of bodily integrity has been embodied in the requirement that informed consent is generally required for medical treatment. Justice [Benjamin] Cardozo, while on the Court of Appeals of New York, aptly described this doctrine: Every human being of adult years and sound mind has a right to determine what shall be done with his own body, and a surgeon who performs an operation without his patient's consent commits an assault, for which he is liable in damages. The informed consent doctrine has become firmly entrenched in American tort law.

Quinlan and Other Cases

The logical corollary of the doctrine of informed consent is that the patient generally possesses the right not to consent, that is, to refuse treatment. Until about 15 years ago and the seminal decision in *In re Quinlan* (1976), the number of right-to-refuse-treatment decisions were relatively few. Most of the earlier cases involved patients who refused medical treatment forbidden by their religious beliefs, thus implicating First Amendment rights as well as common law rights of self-determination. More recently, however, with the advance of medical technology capable of sustaining life well past the point where natural forces would have brought certain death in earlier times, cases involving the right to refuse life-sustaining treatment have burgeoned.

In the *Quinlan* case, young Karen Quinlan suffered severe brain damage as the result of anoxia, and entered a persistent vegetative state. Karen's father sought judicial approval to disconnect his daughter's respirator. The New Jersey Supreme Court granted the relief, holding that Karen had a right of privacy grounded in the Federal Constitution to terminate treatment. Recognizing that this right was not absolute, however, the court balanced it against asserted state interests. Noting that the State's interest "weakens and the individual's right to privacy grows as the degree of bodily invasion increases and the prognosis dims," the court concluded that the state interests had to give way in that case. The court also concluded that the "only practical way" to prevent the loss of Karen's privacy right due to her incompetence was to allow her guardian and family to decide "whether she would exercise it in these circumstances."

After *Quinlan*, however, most courts have based a right to refuse treatment either solely on the common law right to informed consent or on both the common law right and a constitutional privacy right. In *Superintendent of Belchertown State School v. Saikewicz* (1977), the Supreme Judicial Court of Massachusetts relied on both the right of privacy and the right of informed consent to permit the withholding of chemotherapy from a profoundly-retarded 67-year-old man suffering from leukemia. Reasoning that an incompetent person retains the same rights as a competent individual "because the value of human dignity extends to both," the court adopted a "substituted judgment" standard whereby courts were to determine what an incompetent individual's decision would have been under the circumstances. Distilling certain state interests from prior case law—the preservation of life, the protection of the interests of innocent third parties, the prevention of suicide, and the maintenance of the ethical integrity of the medical profession—the court recognized the first interest as paramount and noted it was greatest when an affliction was curable, as opposed to the State interest where, as here, the issue is not whether, but when, for how long, and at what cost to the individual [a] life may be briefly extended.

Doctrine of Informed Consent

In *In re Storar* (1981), the New York Court of Appeals declined to base a right to refuse treatment on a constitutional privacy right. Instead, it found such a right "adequately supported" by the informed consent doctrine. . . . In the case, a 52-year-old man suffering from bladder cancer had been profoundly retarded during most of his life. Implicitly rejecting the approach taken in *Saikewicz, supra*, the court reasoned that, due to such life-long incompetency, "it is unrealistic to attempt to determine whether he would want to continue potentially life-prolonging treatment if he were competent." As the evidence showed that the patient's required blood transfusions did not involve excessive pain and, without them, his mental and physical abilities would deteriorate, the court concluded that it should not allow an incompetent patient to bleed to death because someone, even someone as close as a parent or sibling, feels that this is best for one with an incurable disease.

Many of the later cases build on the principles established in *Quinlan, Saikewicz* and *Storar/Eichner.* For instance, in *In re Conroy* (1985), the same court that decided *Quinlan* considered whether a nasogastric feeding tube could be removed from an 84-year-old incompetent nursing-home resident suffering irreversible mental and physical ailments. While recognizing that a federal right of privacy might apply in the case, the court, contrary to its approach in *Quinlan*, decided to base its decision on the common law right to self-determination and informed consent.

On balance, the right to self-determination ordinarily outweighs any countervailing state interests, and competent persons generally are permitted to refuse medical treatment, even at the risk of death. Most of the cases that have held otherwise, unless they involved the interest in protecting innocent third parties, have concerned the patient's competency to make a rational and considered choice.

Trustworthy Evidence

Reasoning that the right of self-determination should not be lost merely because an individual is unable to sense a violation of it, the court held that incompetent individuals retain a right to refuse treatment. It also held that such a right could be exercised by a surrogate decisionmaker using a "subjective" standard when there was clear evidence that the incompetent person would have exercised it. Where such evidence was lacking, the court held that an individual's right could still be invoked in certain circumstances under objective "best interest" standards. Thus, if some trustworthy evidence existed that the individual would have wanted to terminate treatment, but not enough to clearly establish a person's wishes for purposes of the subjective standard, and the burden of a prolonged life from the experience of pain and suffering markedly outweighed its satisfactions, treatment could be terminated under a "limited-objective" standard. Where no trustworthy evidence existed, and a person's suffering would make the administration of life-sustaining treatment inhumane, a "pure-objective" standard could be used to terminate treatment. If none of these conditions obtained, the court held it was best to err in favor of preserving life.

The court also rejected certain categorical distinctions that had been drawn in prior refusal-of-treatment cases as lacking substance for decision purposes: the distinction between actively hastening death by terminating treatment and passively allowing a person to die of a disease; between treating individuals as an initial matter versus withdrawing treatment afterwards; between ordinary versus extraordinary treatment; and between treatment by artificial feeding versus other forms of life-sustaining medical procedures. As to the last item, the court acknowledged the "emotional significance" of food, but noted that feeding by implanted tubes is a medical procedur[e] with inherent risks and possible side effects, instituted by skilled healthcare providers to compensate for impaired physical functioning which analytically was equivalent to artificial breathing using a respirator.

Patient's Expressed Intent

In contrast to *Conroy*, the Court of Appeals of New York recently refused to accept less than the clearly expressed wishes of a patient before permitting the exercise of her right to refuse treatment by a surrogate decisionmaker (*In re Westchester County Medical Center on behalf of O'Connor* 1988). There, the court, over the objection of the patient's family members, granted an order to insert a feeding tube into a 77-year-old woman rendered incompetent as a result of several strokes. While continuing to recognize a common law right to refuse treatment, the court rejected the substituted judgment approach for asserting it because it is inconsistent with our fundamental commitment to the notion that no person or court should substitute its judgment as to what would be an acceptable quality of life for another. Consequently, we adhere to the view that, despite its pitfalls and inevitable uncertainties, the inquiry must always be narrowed to the patient's expressed intent, with every effort made to minimize the opportunity for error.

The court held that the record lacked the requisite clear and convincing evidence of the patient's expressed intent to withhold life-sustaining treatment. . . .

Clear and Convincing Evidence

Whether or not Missouri's clear and convincing evidence requirement comports with the United States Constitution depends in part on what interests the State may properly seek to protect in this situation. Missouri relies on its interest in the protection and preservation of human life, and there can be no gainsaying this interest. As a general matter, the States—indeed, all civilized nations—demonstrate their commitment to life by treating homicide as serious crime. Moreover, the majority of States in this country have laws imposing criminal penalties on one who assists another to commit suicide. We do not think a State is required to remain neutral in the face of an informed and voluntary decision by a physically able adult to starve to death.

But in the context presented here, a State has more particular interests at stake. The choice between life and death is a deeply personal decision of obvious and overwhelming finality. We believe Missouri may legitimately seek to safeguard the personal element of this choice through the imposition of heightened evidentiary requirements. It cannot be disputed that the Due Process Clause protects an interest in life as well as an interest in refusing life-sustaining medical treatment. Not all incompetent patients will have loved ones available to serve as surrogate decisionmakers. And even where family members are present "[t]here will, of course, be some unfortunate situations in which family members will not act to protect a patient" (*In re Jobes* 1987). A State is entitled to guard against potential abuses in such situations. Similarly, a State is entitled to consider that a judicial proceeding to make a determination regarding an incompetent's wishes may very well not be an adversarial one, with the added guarantee of accurate factfinding that the adversary process brings with it. Finally, we think a State may properly decline to make judgments about the "quality" of life that a particular individual may enjoy, and simply assert an unqualified interest in the preservation of human life to be weighed against the constitutionally protected interests of the individual.

In our view, Missouri has permissibly sought to advance these interests through the adoption of a "clear and convincing" standard of proof to govern such proceedings. . . .

We think it self-evident that the interests at stake in the instant proceedings are more substantial, both on an individual and societal level, than those involved in a run-of-the-mill civil dispute. But not only does the standard of proof reflect the importance of a particular adjudication, it also serves as "a societal judgment about how the risk of error should be distributed between the litigants" (*Santosky v. Kramer* 1982). The more stringent the burden of proof a party must bear, the more that party bears the risk of an erroneous decision. We believe that Missouri may permissibly place an increased risk of an erroneous decision on those seeking to terminate an incompetent individual's life-sustaining treatment. An erroneous decision not to terminate results in a maintenance of the *status quo;* the possibility of subsequent developments such as advancements in medical science, the discovery of new evidence regarding the patient's intent, changes in the law, or simply the unexpected death of the patient despite the administration of life-sustaining treatment, at least create the potential that a wrong decision will eventually be corrected or its impact mitigated. An erroneous decision to withdraw life-sustaining treatment, however, is not susceptible of correction.

No Constitutional Error

In sum, we conclude that a State may apply a clear and convincing evidence standard in proceedings where a guardian seeks to discontinue nutrition and hydration of a person diagnosed to be in a persistent vegetative state. We note that many courts which have adopted some sort of substituted judgment procedure in situations like this, whether they limit consideration of evidence to the prior expressed wishes of the incompetent individual, or whether they allow more general proof of what the individual's decision would have been, require a clear and convincing standard of proof for such evidence. . . .

The Supreme Court of Missouri held that, in this case, the testimony adduced at trial did not amount to clear and convincing proof of the patient's desire to have hydration and nutrition withdrawn. In so doing, it reversed a decision of the Missouri trial court, which had found that the evidence "suggest[ed]" Nancy Cruzan would not have desired to continue such measures, but which had not adopted the standard of "clear and convincing evidence" enunciated by the Supreme Court. The testimony adduced at trial consisted primarily of Nancy Cruzan's statements, made to a housemate about a year before her accident, that she would not want to live should she face life as a "vegetable," and other observations to the same effect. The observations did not deal in terms with withdrawal of medical treatment or of hydration and nutrition. We cannot say that the Supreme Court of Missouri committed constitutional error in reaching the conclusion that it did. . . .

No doubt is engendered by anything in this record but that Nancy Cruzan's mother and father are loving and caring parents. If the State were required by the United States Constitution to repose a right of "substituted judgment" with anyone, the Cruzans would surely qualify. But we do not think the Due Process Clause requires the State to repose judgment on these matters with anyone but the patient herself. Close family members may have a strong feeling—a feeling not at all ignoble or unworthy, but not entirely disinterested, either—that they do not wish to witness the continuation of the life of a loved one which they regard as hopeless, meaningless, and even degrading. But there is no automatic assurance that the view of close family members will necessarily be the same as the patient's would have been had she been confronted with the prospect of her situation while competent. All of the reasons previously discussed for allowing Missouri to require clear and convincing evidence of the patient's wishes lead us to conclude that the State may choose to defer only to those wishes, rather than confide the decision to close family members.

The judgment of the Supreme Court of Missouri is *Affirmed.*

The Hemlock Society Starts the Movement to Legalize Assisted Suicide

DEREK HUMPHRY AND MARY CLEMENT

In the following essay, authors Derek Humphry and Mary Clement discuss the origin and development of the Hemlock Society, which pioneered the movement to legalize assisted suicide for the terminally ill in the United States. In 1980 Humphry established the society, whose purpose was to change existing laws on the prohibition of assisted suicide. To achieve its objective, the society embarked on an information campaign, publishing books and manuals that advocated assisted suicide and described methods to carry it out. Humphry also gave numerous lectures and appeared on many radio and television shows to promote assisted suicide. In 1988 the Hemlock Society sponsored a California ballot initiative to legalize voluntary euthanasia and physician-assisted suicide. Although the initiative failed, it generated greater public awareness of the subject. Humphry has written several books on assisted suicide, including Jean's Way, Final Exit, Let Me Die Before I Wake, *and* The Right to Die *(with Ann Wickett). Clement is coauthor with Humphry of*

Derek Humphry and Mary Clement, *Freedom to Die: People, Politics, and the Right-to-Die Movement.* New York: St. Martin's Press, 1998. Copyright © 1998 by Derek Humphry and Mary Clement. All rights reserved. Reproduced by permission of the publisher.

Freedom to Die: People, Politics, and the Right-to-Die Movement. *A lawyer and expert on right-to-die issues, she is also the author of* How to Die Without a Lawyer *and president of Gentle Closure, Inc., an organization offering assistance to the terminally ill on end-of-life decisions, including assisted suicide. She has provided expert advice on assisted suicide to the U.S. Supreme Court, the Ninth and Second Circuit Courts of Appeals, and the Supreme Court of Alaska.*

The United States was introduced to the idea of medically assisted dying by Derek Humphry, who formed the Hemlock Society in 1980 and in the following twelve years built it from an unknown organization—initially regarded by many as distinctly oddball—operated from his garage on 32nd Street, Santa Monica, into a nationally recognized force for social change on the issue of the right to choose to die. His tools were his books on the subject and skills in public relations acquired during thirty-five years as a journalist. He knew how to talk to journalists, and could write quick press releases and advertising copy. Journalists respected him for having worked at all levels of journalism, from local weeklies to giant international journals. Humphry was also an experienced broadcaster on radio and television.

A personal tragedy with his first wife, Jean, had introduced him to assisted suicide and eventually led to his forming Hemlock to work to change the law. . . . Jean contracted breast cancer that rapidly metastasized into bone cancer. Radical mastectomy, removal of the lymph nodes (already affected), chemotherapy, and radiation all failed to check the cancer. Within a year Derek knew she was dying and that the end was only a matter of time. . . .

When Derek returned to Churchill Hospital [in Oxford, England] one day, he found Jean sitting up in bed. . . . His epiphany was at hand.

"Derek," she said, taking a deep breath, "I simply don't

want to go on living like this. It's been pretty bad this week and I want you to do something for me so that if I decide I want to die I can do it on my own terms and exactly when I choose. The one thing that worries me is that I won't be in any position to make the right decision, what with my being knocked senseless by all these drugs. I might be too daft to know whether I'm doing the right thing or not but I shall have a good idea when I've had enough of the pain. So I want you to promise me that when I ask you if this is the right time to kill myself, you will give me an honest answer one way or another and we must understand, both you and I, that I'll do it right at that very moment. You won't question my right and you will give me the means to do it."

After a pause to absorb this surprising request, Derek told her that if their positions were reversed and he was the one dying of cancer, he would be asking Jean to help him die. It was an instinctive reply, because he had never previously considered the matter. Like many other couples in their early forties, thoughts of death, and of how dying might be handled, had not been considered. At the time he had no idea that this brief conversation would eventually completely alter the rest of his life. Almost immediately Derek sought out a physician in London who had been helpful to him some years previously when he was doing investigative reporting on administrative problems in the British National Health Service.

"Dr. Joe"—which is the only clue Derek has ever revealed to his identity—heard his plea for lethal drugs with which Jean could kill herself. He questioned him closely about her medical condition and concluded: "She has no quality of life left." Almost casually Dr. Joe telephoned the chief pharmacist at the hospital where he had privileges and asked which drugs would be most lethal in these circumstances. The conversation over, and reluctant to write out a prescription that could give him away to the authorities, he went to his drugs cabinet and gave Derek two substances, with instructions how to use them. "Never reveal that I did this," instructed Dr. Joe. The two men shook hands.

Both were about to commit the crime of assisted suicide under Section 2 of the Suicide Act of 1961, making them liable of conviction for up to fourteen years' imprisonment. The same act stipulated that Jean's suicide was no longer a felony; thus the two men were technically perpetrating a crime, but only to carry out something that was not a crime—a distinction that struck Derek as ludicrous. But immediately after Jean's request, he studied this particular law and noticed a caveat in it. A prosecution could not be directly brought by the police—as with most crimes—but only with the permission of the Director of Public Prosecutions. Having written about the administration of justice for the *Sunday Times* for many years, Derek knew that the current director was a man of humane and liberal tendencies. So he decided that the necessity of helping Jean to die was worth the small risk of prosecution. . . .

Nine months elapsed between the making of the assisted suicide pact and Jean's death, but it was never discussed between the couple, although Jean would occasionally tell her women friends that she was "not planning to go to the end with this." Apparently these friends, who knew Jean's determined character, accepted these remarks and remembered them. These fairly offhand statements turned out to be fortuitous for Derek when the police went looking for evidence against him three years later. It showed that the suicide had been Jean's plan and not Derek's.

In March 1975 Jean's cancer returned with a vengeance, spreading from her bones to her vital organs. Back in the hospital, her doctors told her that there were no more treatments available for her condition. They promised to manage her pain and offered her the choice between dying in a hospital or at home. With her self-deliverance plan in mind, she opted for an ambulance to take her home. Accompanying her was a large bottle of what the British call "Brompton cocktail" and Americans call "hospice mix," which is a concoction of narcotic analgesics made up by trial and error to quell the pain of an individual patient. In overdose it is lethal, and could have been used in Jean's suicide instead of Dr. Joe's pills. . . .

When she awoke on March 29, Jean's pain was so intense that she was unable to move. Derek brought her painkillers, and once they had taken effect she was able to sit up cautiously in bed, propped up by numerous pillows.

"Is this the day?" Jean quietly asked Derek.

For a few moments he was paralyzed by the awesome nature of the question. She had decided to die. Although not unexpected, it was nevertheless traumatic to have to give permission to the person whom he loved most in the world to kill herself. Part of their original pact had been that Jean would not act without her husband's agreement; now he had to decide whether he concurred. He temporized for a moment by discussing Jean's present worsening condition, which might necessitate a quick return to the hospital, and then conceded that perhaps the time had come.

Sensing his acceptance, Jean immediately said: "I shall die at one o'clock. You must give me the overdose and then go into the garden and not return for an hour. We'll say our last goodbye here, but I don't want you actually to see me die."

As one o'clock approached, a calm and collected Jean asked Derek to get her the drugs, which he had decided would be best taken in a large mug of coffee with a lot of milk, plentifully laced with sugar to reduce the bitter taste of the barbiturates and codeine.

After the couple embraced for the last time, Jean's last words were "Goodbye my love." She immediately took the mug and gulped its contents swiftly. Derek ignored her request to leave the room, considering it better to ensure that nothing went wrong. Within seconds the drugs had knocked Jean out and she lay breathing heavily. At one point Jean vomited—the couple did not know of the importance of antiemetics to prevent sickness caused by swallowing so much medication—and Derek was terrified that she had not kept down enough of the deadly potion.

He prepared himself to stifle her with a pillow if she showed signs of awakening because he had given his word that she would not awaken. Fortunately for both of them within fifty minutes the drugs worked and respiration stopped completely. Jean lay peacefully at rest after all her suffering; Derek sat at her bedside dazed by the loss yet also filled with admiration for the courageous, determined, and dignified manner of her death. . . .

Writing a Book

After a period of mourning, Derek took Jean's deathbed advice to get on with his life as soon as possible. During her illness Derek had not considered writing about it, although some of his colleagues had suggested his doing so. But, as he gradually managed to distance himself from the sadness of her death, he thought about writing a long magazine article about the experience of helping a loved one to die.

Following his marriage to Ann Wickett, a year later, his new wife urged him to write a book about Jean's life and death, and she offered to help. An American who had studied psychology at Boston and Toronto Universities, and now a student at England's Shakespeare Institute, Ann was able to provide and express certain insights he could not. . . .

When *Jean's Way* hit the bookstores in March 1978 it immediately sold out, earning a wave of publicity, nationally and internationally, considerably helped by a powerful television documentary shown on London Weekend Television. Suddenly Derek found himself defending assisted suicide in public. . . .

After the media had no more angles for stories on Derek within a few days, they asked the director of public prosecutions what he was going to do about this clear confession to a crime in *Jean's Way*. He ordered a police inquiry so that he could—as the 1961 Suicide Act allowed—make a decision on whether to prosecute. . . .

The police found that this accelerated death was entirely Jean's plan, with Derek as a mere accessory. Six months later the public prosecutor ruled that he was exercising the discretion allowed him by law and would not prosecute. . . .

After the U.S. publication of *Jean's Way* in 1979, Derek was invited on all the major talk shows, television and radio, although the book sold modestly. But the visibility was enormous for what was now developing into a major cause for Derek. . . .

Setting the Stage for Legislation

The idea was developing in Derek's mind that there ought to be an organization, similar to those in Britain and Australia, fighting for Americans' right to a chosen death. First he approached the two right-to-die groups in New York, Concern for Dying and the Society for the Right to Die (now merged as Choice in Dying) and asked them to branch out from advance directives into physician-assisted suicide. They declined, claiming that the United States was not ready for this. They were only interested in what is known as "passive euthanasia"—the disconnection of life-support systems in hopeless cases. Derek felt they were wrong not to extend their field because for him the evidence indicated a high degree of interest. He talked with Ann about his plan for a specialized group. She suggested it be called "Hemlock," and he agreed, adding "Society" as a clarification of what it was. Thus was born the Hemlock Society, America's first group to fight exclusively to change the law on assisted suicide for the terminally ill. . . .

At the height of the rumpus over *Jean's Way* in London in 1978, the *Evening Standard* had asked Derek for a feature-page article that appeared under the headline of THE RIGHT TO DIE WITH DIGNITY. In the article Derek, though a novice in this field, presented a four-point charter for legislation:

1. The patient must know the essentials of his situation, the available therapies, the alternative prognosis and possibilities. He must be fully aware that euthanasia is irreversible death.

2. The patient must have voluntarily requested euthana-

sia, preferably repeatedly, confirming that the present situation and all available alternatives are unbearable to him.

3. He must be incurable, with no possibility of alleviating his suffering in a manner acceptable to him. Death must, in his informed and considered opinion, be the only acceptable solution.

4. Euthanasia must be applied by the attending doctor.

Making allowances for the then poorly defined meaning of words such as "euthanasia," this appears to have been the first published charter for assisted suicide in the English-speaking world. (The Dutch had been working on such propositions for the previous five years.) Developing his original ideas, Derek two years later drew up a draft charter for the aims and objects of Hemlock, circulating it to dozens of legal and health professionals in California whom he knew were interested in the subject. In essence it said that Hemlock would provide information so that people who were dying could end their own lives with dignity, and, in the long term, Hemlock would fight for a reform of the law. It would be a nonprofit California educational corporation with a board of directors and a small staff.

In California, where the national organization was to be based from the outset, suicide was not a crime, but under Penal Code 401 any form of assistance was felonious, punishable by up to five years' imprisonment. As much as Derek researched, he could not find a single instance of an assisted suicide conviction since the law had been passed in 1897. Although some warned him against starting what critics would label a crazy pro-suicide club, he relied on his public relations skills to get it across to the law enforcement authorities and the public that this was assistance only for the terminally ill and the irreversibly ill purely on a voluntary basis, with a long-term aim of democratic law reform to permit the procedure under regulated circumstances. Thirty-two other states had specific laws punishing assistance in suicide, while the remainder considered it murder or manslaughter. Law reform on this scale, with such a controversial issue, was obviously a mountainous task, but Derek told supporters from the start that it would probably take twenty years to achieve.

The original draft charter—or mission statement—of Hemlock read as follows:

Charter Principles, 1980

1. Hemlock's objective is to promote a climate of public opinion which is tolerant of the right of people who are terminally ill to end their own lives in a planned manner.

2. Hemlock does not condone suicide for any primary emotional, traumatic or financial reasons in the absence of terminal illness. It approves of the work of all those involved in suicide prevention.

3. Hemlock will not encourage terminally ill people to end their lives, believing this action, and its timing, to be an extremely personal decision, wherever possible taken in concert with family and friends.

4. A book providing information about methods and strategies of planned death with dignity will be supplied to members upon request. (This book is in preparation and not immediately available.)

5. Hemlock speaks only to those people of like mind who approach it out of mutual sympathy with its goals. Views contrary to its own which are held by other religions and philosophies are respected. . . .

Derek now set out to provide: a book on how to end one's life through the use of drugs. Richard Scott [a physician and lawyer interested in Derek's plans], who joined Hemlock's board of directors once he had seen that its public reception had escaped problems, advised him to get true accounts of terminally ill people's own suicides and report them in great detail in a book. His advice was that, in the United States, a writer could not be sued or prosecuted for telling the truth. Within the stories should be given the exact quantities of drugs ingested and the consequences.

Hemlock appealed to all its members for personal stories of helping another to die. The response was huge, and soon Derek had all the material he needed to write *Let Me Die Before I Wake.* . . .

When the book first appeared in 1981, Hemlock, out of caution, confined it to members only. However, protests came from some in the book trade that this was "not the American way," so at the start of 1982 the book was thrown open to libraries and sale in stores. It attracted very little media attention, which at that time did not take assisted dying with much seriousness. But right-to-die supporters for the next ten years bought it at the rate of approximately twenty-five thousand copies a year. . . .

Throughout the 1980s, when the right to die was a low-priority public policy issue, Hemlock organized national conferences that attracted considerable attention from the public and media.

Gradually, Hemlock came to be widely known, even if not accepted, throughout the United States. Derek's main avenue for securing visibility for the cause was talk radio. He employed the long-established Hollywood radio publicist Irwin Zucker to get him bookings on shows. In a busy year Derek talked on as many as three hundred shows, at the end of each broadcast giving out Hemlock's address and telephone number. The partnership between him and Zucker was a fruitful one. Talk-show hosts discovered that the right-to-die topic attracted plenty of listeners, with abundant call-ins; everybody had a view on the matter, a question, or a horror story to tell of a loved one's death. Derek averaged about twenty-five television shows, local and national, in a year, using his books as the entrée. . . .

In 1985, as public acceptance grew larger, the organization became bolder and started publishing drug charts in its newsletter, *Hemlock Quarterly*, and sending reprints for two dollars to all who wrote and asked. The membership, only a small percentage of whom were terminally ill, was always hungry for information on lethal drugs and how to get them. They had no intention of suiciding now, but knew that the time may come. The newsletter catered to this demand whenever possible. How many terminally ill people ended their lives with the information in *Let Me Die Before I Wake* and the newsletter will never be known, although Derek estimates that it was in the thousands over a period of ten years.

By 1987 Hemlock's membership totaled fifteen thousand. Within two years it had doubled. The reason for the spurt in growth was the attempt to qualify a ballot initiative in California in 1988, which, if it had passed, would have legalized voluntary euthanasia and physician-assisted suicide for terminally ill adults. The attempt failed miserably in terms of signatures gathered because Hemlock, and its political arm, Americans Against Human Suffering (renamed, in 1993, Americans for Death with Dignity), lacked the money to finance paid signature gathering, which is essential in such a huge state as California, where some four hundred thousand signatures are required to get on the ballot. But the publicity surrounding the attempt, particularly the scrutiny given to the wording of the first such law ever published, was so large that supporters who had been previously unaware of Hemlock enrolled in droves.

The Supreme Court Upholds a State's Ban on Assisted Suicide

WILLIAM REHNQUIST

In 1997 the Supreme Court ruled on two cases that led it to address, for the first time, the question of assisted suicide. The first case, known as Glucksberg v. Washington, *began in 1994 in Washington State, where an organization supporting euthanasia filed a suit against the state. The second case, known as* Quill v. Vacco, *was filed in July 1994 in New York. In both cases, a group of physicians and terminally ill patients sued the state, claiming that the prohibition against assisted suicide violated the due process and equal protection rights guaranteed by the U.S. Constitution. Both cases went through reversals in the lower courts and reached the Supreme Court, which made a final ruling in 1997. In the following selection, Chief Justice William Rehnquist presents the high court's ruling on* Quill, *denying a constitutional right to assisted suicide even for terminally ill, mentally competent adults. The Court reaffirms the state's interest in preserving life and preventing suicide and accepts the view of the American Medical Association that assisted suicide subverts a physician's role and could harm vulnerable groups. The Court also directs the states to conduct further debate on the subject in their re-*

William Rehnquist, majority opinion, *Dennis C. Vacco, Attorney General of New York et al., Petitioners v. Timothy E. Quill et al.*, U.S. Supreme Court, June 26, 1997.

spective legislatures. Rehnquist was appointed chief justice by President Ronald Reagan in 1986.

In New York, as in most States, it is a crime to aid another to commit or attempt suicide, but patients may refuse even lifesaving medical treatment. The question presented by this case is whether New York's prohibition on assisting suicide therefore violates the Equal Protection Clause of the [U.S. Constitution's] Fourteenth Amendment. We hold that it does not.

Petitioners are various New York public officials. Respondents [those against whom an appeal is taken] Timothy E. Quill, Samuel C. Klagsbrun, and Howard A. Grossman are physicians who practice in New York. They assert that although it would be "consistent with the standards of [their] medical practice[s]" to prescribe lethal medication for "mentally competent, terminally ill patients" who are suffering great pain and desire a doctor's help in taking their own lives, they are deterred from doing so by New York's ban on assisting suicide. [The physician respondents] and three gravely ill patients who have since died, sued the State's Attorney General in the United States District Court. They urged that because New York permits a competent person to refuse life sustaining medical treatment, and because the refusal of such treatment is "essentially the same thing" as physician assisted suicide, New York's assisted suicide ban violates the Equal Protection Clause.

The District Court disagreed: "[I]t is hardly unreasonable or irrational for the State to recognize a difference between allowing nature to take its course, even in the most severe situations, and intentionally using an artificial death producing device." The court noted New York's "obvious legitimate interests in preserving life, and in protecting vulnerable persons," and concluded that "[u]nder the United States Constitution and the federal system it establishes, the resolution of this issue is left to the normal democratic processes within the State."

The Court of Appeals for the Second Circuit reversed. The court determined that, despite the assisted suicide ban's apparent general applicability, "New York law does not treat equally all competent persons who are in the final stages of fatal illness and wish to hasten their deaths," because "those in the final stages of terminal illness who are on life support systems are allowed to hasten their deaths by directing the removal of such systems; but those who are similarly situated, except for the previous attachment of life sustaining equipment, are not allowed to hasten death by self administering prescribed drugs." In the court's view, "[t]he ending of life by [the withdrawal of life support systems] is *nothing more nor less than assisted suicide*." The Court of Appeals then examined whether this supposed unequal treatment was rationally related to any legitimate state interests, and concluded that "to the extent that [New York's statutes] prohibit a physician from prescribing medications to be self administered by a mentally competent, terminally ill person in the final stages of his terminal illness, they are not rationally related to any legitimate state interest."

The Equal Protection Clause commands that no State shall "deny to any person within its jurisdiction the equal protection of the laws." This provision creates no substantive rights. Instead, it embodies a general rule that States must treat like cases alike but may treat unlike cases accordingly. . . .

On their faces, neither New York's ban on assisting suicide nor its statutes permitting patients to refuse medical treatment treat anyone differently than anyone else or draw any distinctions between persons. *Everyone*, regardless of physical condition, is entitled, if competent, to refuse unwanted lifesaving medical treatment; *no one* is permitted to assist a suicide. Generally speaking, laws that apply evenhandedly to all "unquestionably comply" with the Equal Protection Clause. . . .

The Court of Appeals, however, concluded that some

terminally ill people—those who are on life support systems—are treated differently than those who are not, in
that the former may "hasten death" by ending treatment,
but the latter may not "hasten death" through physician
assisted suicide. This conclusion depends on the submis-
sion that ending or refusing lifesaving medical treatment
"is nothing more nor less than assisted suicide." Unlike the
Court of Appeals, we think the distinction between assisting suicide and withdrawing life sustaining treatment, a distinction widely recognized and endorsed in the medical
profession and in our legal traditions, is both important
and logical; it is certainly rational.

The distinction comports with fundamental legal principles of causation and intent. First, when a patient refuses
life sustaining medical treatment, he dies from an underlying fatal disease or pathology; but if a patient ingests lethal
medication prescribed by a physician, he is killed by that
medication. . . .

Furthermore, a physician who withdraws, or honors a
patient's refusal to begin, life sustaining medical treatment
purposefully intends, or may so intend, only to respect his
patient's wishes and "to cease doing useless and futile or
degrading things to the patient when [the patient] no
longer stands to benefit from them," according to the testimony of Dr. Leon R. Kass. The same is true when a doctor
provides aggressive palliative care; in some cases, painkilling drugs may hasten a patient's death, but the physician's purpose and intent is, or may be, only to ease his patient's pain. A doctor who assists a suicide, however,
"must, necessarily and indubitably, intend primarily that
the patient be made dead." Similarly, a patient who commits suicide with a doctor's aid necessarily has the specific
intent to end his or her own life, while a patient who refuses or discontinues treatment might not. . . .

The law has long used actors' intent or purpose to distinguish between two acts that may have the same result.
Put differently, the law distinguishes actions taken "be-

cause of" a given end from actions taken "in spite of" their unintended but foreseen consequences. . . .

Given these general principles, it is not surprising that many courts, including New York courts, have carefully distinguished refusing life sustaining treatment from suicide. . . .

Similarly, the overwhelming majority of state legislatures have drawn a clear line between assisting suicide and withdrawing or permitting the refusal of unwanted lifesaving medical treatment by prohibiting the former and permitting the latter. And "nearly all states expressly disapprove of suicide and assisted suicide either in statutes dealing with durable powers of attorney in health care situations, or in 'living will' statutes" [*People v. Kevorkian* (1994)].

The Case of New York

New York is a case in point. The State enacted its current assisted suicide statutes in 1965. Since then, New York has acted several times to protect patients' common law right to refuse treatment. In so doing, however, the State has neither endorsed a general right to "hasten death" nor approved physician assisted suicide. Quite the opposite: The State has reaffirmed the line between "killing" and "letting die." More recently, the New York State Task Force on Life and the Law studied assisted suicide and euthanasia and, in 1994, unanimously recommended against legalization. In the Task Force's view, "allowing decisions to forego life sustaining treatment and allowing assisted suicide or euthanasia have radically different consequences and meanings for public policy."

This Court has also recognized, at least implicitly, the distinction between letting a patient die and making that patient die. In *Cruzan v. Director, Mo. Dept. of Health* [involving the removal of a feeding tube from a patient] (1990), we concluded that "[t]he principle that a competent person has a constitutionally protected liberty interest in refusing unwanted medical treatment may be inferred from our prior decisions," and we assumed the existence of such a right for purposes of that case. But our assumption of a right to refuse treatment was grounded not, as the Court of Appeals supposed, on the proposition that patients have a general and abstract "right to hasten death," but on well established, traditional rights to bodily integrity and freedom from unwanted touching. In fact, we observed that "the majority of States in this country have laws imposing criminal penalties on one who assists another to commit suicide." *Cruzan* therefore provides no support for the notion that refusing life sustaining medical treatment is "nothing more nor less than suicide."

For all these reasons, we disagree with respondents' claim that the distinction between refusing lifesaving medical treatment and assisted suicide is "arbitrary" and "irrational." Granted, in some cases, the line between the two may not be clear, but certainty is not required, even were it possible. Logic and contemporary practice support New York's judgment that the two acts are different, and New York may therefore, consistent with the Constitution, treat them differently. By permitting everyone to refuse unwanted medical treatment while prohibiting anyone from assisting a suicide, New York law follows a longstanding and rational distinction.

New York's reasons for recognizing and acting on this distinction—including prohibiting intentional killing and preserving life; preventing suicide; maintaining physicians' role as their patients' healers; protecting vulnerable people from indifference, prejudice, and psychological and financial pressure to end their lives; and avoiding a possible slide towards euthanasia—are discussed in greater detail in our opinion in *Washington v. Glucksberg* (1997). These valid and important public interests easily satisfy the constitutional requirement that a legislative classification bear a rational relation to some legitimate end.

The judgment of the Court of Appeals is reversed.

Assisted Suicide Could Be Legalized in the Future

RONALD DWORKIN

In the following article, law professor Ronald Dworkin analyzes the 1997 Supreme Court rejection of a constitutional right to assisted suicide in New York and Washington. He states that some of the justices rejected the right not on principle, but because of concerns that the practice of assisted suicide would be difficult to regulate and could lead to discrimination against vulnerable groups. This reasoning suggests that the Court could change its opinion in the future when it has more evidence of the practical impact of assisted suicide. Dworkin points out that the tentativeness of the Court's ruling augurs well for more debate and possible future acceptance of a right to assisted suicide. Dworkin is a professor of philosophy and law at New York University. He is also a professor of jurisprudence at Oxford University and a fellow at University College in London. A euthanasia advocate, he is the lead author of the Philosophers' Brief, *submitted to the Supreme Court in aid for its ruling in the 1997 cases. He is the author of several books, including* Law's Empire; Sovereign Virtue: The Theory and Practice of Equality; Life's Dominion: An Argument About Abortion, Euthanasia, and Individual Freedom; *and* Freedom's Law: The Moral Reading of the American Constitution.

Ronald Dworkin, "Assisted Suicide: What the Court Really Said," *The New York Review of Books*, vol. 44, no. 14, September 25, 1997. Copyright © 1997 by NYREV, Inc. Reproduced by permission.

In March 1997 six moral and political philosophers [submitted an amicus curiae brief] to the Supreme Court urging the Court, in cases then pending, to recognize a limited constitutional right of terminally ill and competent patients to the help of a doctor in ending their lives, in order to avoid further pointless suffering and anguish. On June 26 the Court decided these cases refusing to recognize such a right by an apparently cruising 9-0 vote. But though press reports did not make this clear, the unanimity of the vote was deceptive. Five of the six justices who wrote opinions made it plain that they did not reject such a right in principle, suggesting that the Court might well change its mind in a future case when more evidence of the practical impact of any such right was available.

The cases raised, moreover, not only the question of a specific right to assisted suicide, but a more fundamental constitutional issue as well—how to understand and enforce the "due process clause" of the Fourteenth Amendment, which declares that states may not "deprive any person of life, liberty or property, without due process of law." That clause offers more potential protection to the liberty of individual citizens than any other constitutional provision. Its language is very abstract, however, and the actual protection it offers depends on whether it is read narrowly or expansively. . . .

In his majority opinion in the assisted suicide cases, on behalf of himself and four other justices, Chief Justice William Rehnquist defended an historicist view of the "Nation's history and tradition" test. He insisted that the due process clause protects only those specific liberties that have historically been respected by American states, so that the clause does protect citizens from unwanted and invasive medical treatment, because the common law of most states has for a long time granted that protection. But, according to Rehnquist, the clause permits laws prohibiting a doctor from helping people dying in great pain to die sooner, because almost all states have long prohibited such help.

In an unusually candid statement of this view, Rehnquist acknowledged that it might well produce anomalies of principle, because it might well be that no principled distinction can be drawn between liberties that American states have historically protected and those that they have denied. He said that the Supreme Court's suggestion, in its earlier *Cruzan* decision, that the due process clause gives people a right to have life-saving apparatus removed from their bodies was drawn only from common-law practice, and was

> not simply deduced from abstract concepts of personal autonomy. . . . The decision to commit suicide with the assistance of another may be just as personal and profound as the decision to refuse unwanted medical treatment, but it has never enjoyed similar legal protection.

Justice Souter's Opinion

Justice David Souter, on the other hand, in his separate opinion concurring in but not joining Rehnquist's majority opinion, offered a much more expansive view of the historical test. He said that the nation's history and traditions include not just the specific rights that have been recognized in the past, but the "basic values" that are revealed when we interpret those rights to see which more general principles of political morality they represent. It may be, he said, that states have not always been wholly faithful to those basic values, and that some of even the oldest legal practices, like the long prohibition on abortion, can now be seen to offend them and so to violate the due process clause.

Judges, he said, must take care in deciding which principles of political morality do underlie the nation's history, because these values can be identified at varying levels of generality and judges must not state them more broadly than a sound interpretation would justify. He conceded that identifying principles at the right level of generality is not a mechanical matter. "Selecting among such competing characterizations demands reasoned judgment about which broader principle, as exemplified in the concrete privileges and prohibitions embodied in our legal tradition, best fits the particular claim asserted in a particular case." He drew, from his understanding of the due process clause, very different conclusions about assisted suicide from Rehnquist's. If we apply reasoned judgment to the assisted suicide issue, Souter argued, we can identify arguments of what he called "increasing forcefulness for recognizing some right to a doctor's help in suicide."

The strongest of these arguments, he said, rests on a general principle, embedded in past traditions, that guarantees a

> right to medical care and counsel, subject to the limiting conditions of informed, responsible choice when death is imminent. . . . There can be no stronger claim to a physician's assistance than at the time when death is imminent, a moral judgment implied by the State's own recognition of the legitimacy of medical procedures necessarily hastening the moment of impending death [e.g., terminating life support and allowing pain relief that advances death].

The Justices' Differing Views of Due Process

So Rehnquist's and Souter's views of the due process clause are dramatically different: the first protects individuals only from laws that few states have seen any reason to enact, and offers no protection at all against historically popular invasions of individual freedom. The second holds out the possibility that even longstanding and popular legal rules, like the ban on assisted suicide, might be held unconstitutional when they can be seen to violate more general and established principles of freedom.

It is therefore important to try to gauge the popularity of each of these views in the present Supreme Court. Rehnquist, as I have said, had no difficulty in using his historicist approach to reject any right to assisted suicide out of hand. Four other justices—Justices Anthony Kennedy, San-

dra Day O'Connor, Antonin Scalia, and Clarence Thomas—
joined Rehnquist's opinion, and we may safely assume that
Scalia and Thomas do in fact embrace the historicist as-
sumptions of that opinion.

O'Connor and Kennedy, however, were two of the three
justices—the other was Souter—who wrote a joint opinion
in the 1992 *Casey* abortion decision endorsing the inter-
pretive view of due process that Souter defended in this
case, and it is therefore puzzling why they joined Rehnquist's opinion. Perhaps they did so out of institutional
courtesy, so that one opinion—Rehnquist's—could attract
five votes and so count as the opinion of the Court, avoiding the inelegant result of a unanimous decision with no
majority opinion.

In any case, however, O'Connor wrote a separate opinion which makes it plain that she still does not accept
Rehnquist's historicist understanding of the due process
clause. She identified the question posed by the cases as
"whether a mentally competent person who is experiencing great suffering has a constitutionally cognizable interest in controlling the circumstances of his or her imminent
death." She said that she saw no need to decide that question because, even if such a patient had such a right, the
state laws challenged in the cases did not violate it because
they allowed doctors to administer pain-relieving drugs
even when these hastened death. She left open, that is, the
crucial question—whether patients have some right to
control how they die—that the historicist understanding
would have answered, negatively and immediately. Kennedy did not write a separate opinion. But it is unlikely that
he accepts the historicist account, given . . . his opinion in
Casey. . . .

The Dissenting View

Justices Breyer, Ginsburg, and Stevens, who declined to
join Rehnquist's opinion, each made it at least as plain as
O'Connor did that they were much closer to Souter's than

to Rehnquist's understanding of the due process clause. Ginsburg said simply that she agreed with O'Connor. Breyer said pointedly that he joined O'Connor's opinion "except insofar as it joins the majority." He added that he would formulate the patient's claim in these cases, not as Rehnquist had, but rather in "words roughly like a 'right to die with dignity,'" and he said that "our legal tradition may provide greater support" for such a right.

Breyer said, however, that he did not have to decide the question whether the due process clause actually does require judges to recognize such a right, because "the avoidance of severe physical pain (connected with death) would have to comprise an essential part of any successful claim," and he agreed with O'Connor that pain can be avoided because the states do not prohibit even pain-relieving treatment that advances death. He concluded with the important observation that if states did interfere with the "administration of drugs as needed to avoid pain at the end of life," then "as Justice O'Connor suggests, the Court might have to revisit its conclusions in these cases."

The remaining justice—Stevens—wrote an eloquent separate opinion to explain that his vote to reverse the lower court decisions was based on procedural rather than substantive grounds. He said that since the patients who were plaintiffs in the cases at hand had all died before the Supreme Court decision, the question before the Court was not whether the anti-assisted suicide laws could constitutionally be applied to patients who were dying when they asked for relief. Instead, he said, once the patients had died, the case required the Court to decide whether the anti-suicide laws could constitutionally be applied to anyone at all, including, for example, a depressed but otherwise healthy person who had expressed a wish to die. Since he thought that a state could properly prevent doctors from aiding some people who wanted to die, he voted to sustain the statutes as not "facially" invalid.

His opinion left little doubt, however, that in what he

deemed an appropriate case he would vote to overrule a statute that prevented doctors from helping competent and informed dying patients—not just those whose pain could not otherwise be relieved—to die sooner. He emphasized, as the Philosophers' Brief had, that different people have different religious and ethical convictions about what kind of death most respects the value of their life, and that individual freedom demands that dying patients be permitted to die according to their own convictions. He ended with the uncompromising statement that

> In my judgment. . .it is clear that [the states'] so-called "unqualified interest in the preservation of human life" . . . is not itself sufficient to outweigh the interest in liberty that may justify the only possible means of preserving a dying patient's dignity and alleviating her intolerable suffering.

Stevens's opinion, though technically a vote against those who challenged the prohibitory statutes, was in fact a vote for all that they asked.

Future Constitutional Debate Is Left Open

So the narrow, historicist view of the due process clause is now probably confined to a core group of the three most conservative members of the present Court—Rehnquist, Scalia, and Thomas—and that is welcome news for those who favor a principled construction of the individual rights that American citizens enjoy against their government. It is also welcome news that though the Supreme Court refused to recognize a right to assisted suicide in these cases, five justices took care not to foreclose the constitutional debate over such a right for the future.

Stevens's opinion declared his readiness to recognize that right whenever an appropriate case arose. Souter's opinion said three times that his vote was only "at this time." O'Connor and Breyer each said that changed circumstances might cause them to reconsider. And Ginsburg, joining O'Connor's opinion rather than that of the Court, made it clear that she agreed. It is therefore important to consider why each of these justices, except Stevens, declined to recognize the right "at this time."

O'Connor, Ginsburg, and Breyer argued, as I have said, that any constitutional right would be limited to relief from pain. But that limitation seems arbitrary, for several reasons. These justices did not explain why what Breyer called a right to die "with dignity" means only dying without pain when, as Souter noted, many people dread a drug-induced stupor just as much, and understandably think it just as offensive to their dignity. Though these justices declared themselves satisfied that pain could be prevented in all but a very few cases, moreover, they did not attempt to respond to the substantial evidence, cited by Stevens, to the contrary. And it seems odd that they should be ready to overrule carefully considered decisions of the lower federal courts recognizing a limited right to assisted suicide by appealing to a factual claim vigorously contested in the briefs without any argument for that claim.

Nor did these justices explain why those individuals whose pain concededly cannot be relieved except by rendering them unconscious, no matter how few or many they are, do not have a right to assistance in dying. Breyer did acknowledge that many patients, particularly poor patients, do not receive the palliative treatment, which is often expensive, that would benefit them. But, he said, that is for "institutional reasons or inadequacies or obstacles, which would seem possible to overcome." It is unsatisfactory, however, to argue that even if dying poor patients have a right not to die in extreme pain, a state may nevertheless forbid them the assistance of a doctor in suicide, even when that means that they actually will die in great pain because the state refuses to pay for the pain relief that would help them if it were provided.

Souter offered a more elaborate and impressive set of reasons for not recognizing any constitutional right at this time. He mentioned the arguments, pressed by opponents of assisted suicide, that it would prove impossible to design any system of regulatory control that would protect people whose death was not in fact imminent, or who did not really wish to die, from being coaxed into suicide by relatives or hospitals who did not want to bear the expense of keeping them alive, or by compassionate doctors who thought them better off dead. He cited, in particular, books and articles purporting to show that the only documented program of assisted suicide and euthanasia—the Dutch one—had failed to prevent many such mistakes. He noted, however, that these analyses of the Dutch case were contradicted by other reports, and that many writers did think that states could develop an effective regulatory scheme that would reduce mistakes to the level that was unavoidable in any grave medical procedure. But, he said, judges should not declare laws enacted by almost all the states unconstitutional on the basis of disputed and controversial judgments of fact, particularly in circumstances when legislatures, who can deploy investigative committees, are in a better position to assess the facts than judges are. So, he concluded, the Court should not declare anti-assisted suicide laws unconstitutional "at this time," though it might be right to do so later, when and if better evidence is available or more persuasive studies have been made.

That seems reasonable in principle. But, as Souter candidly acknowledged, the Court has assumed that dying patients have a constitutional right to terminate life support even when this means that they will die immediately; and there is as much danger that such patients will be coaxed into a request to die in that way as by requesting lethal pills, particularly since life-support techniques are typically very expensive. In any case, the question whether a factual issue is too difficult or uncertain for judges to decide, so that they ought to defer to legislative decisions for that reason, is itself a complex and difficult one, and the courts should answer it only after very careful review of the evidence, particularly when putatively fundamental rights of individual citizens are at stake. Careful review would seem particularly crucial, moreover, in the assisted suicide debate, because many of the social scientists who have compiled the relevant evidence have strong ethical opinions, including religious convictions, or convictions about proper medical ethics, that might impair their scientific independence.

It is hard to resist the conclusion that those justices who, like Souter, accept an interpretivist rather than an historicist understanding of the due process clause, but who were understandably reluctant to invalidate the laws of almost every state, were unable to find convincing arguments to justify their decision not to do so. That makes it even more likely that the constitutional debate will continue.

What effects will the Court's decisions have in the meantime? The Court made plain that citizens are free to press for permissive reforms in the present law in the ordinary way, through legislation or referendums, and, since the idea that dying patients should have a chance for a doctor's help in easing their death remains popular, such efforts might well succeed in some further states.

The Continuing Legal Battle over Physician-Assisted Suicide in Oregon

LAWRENCE RUDDEN

In November 1994 voters in Oregon passed a measure called the Death with Dignity Act to legalize assisted suicide, but opponents of the measure blocked its implementation. A federal district court pronounced the law unconstitutional in 1995. The law's supporters appealed the ruling, and in February 1997, a panel of the U.S. Ninth Circuit Court of Appeals reversed the lower court's decision, paving the way for the law to take effect. In November 2001, Attorney General John Ashcroft issued a directive penalizing doctors who prescribe painkillers with the intent of ending a patient's life. Ashcroft also warned that doctors who administer lethal injections are violating the Controlled Substances Act and will lose their license and serve a mandatory twenty-year sentence. In the following selection, Lawrence Rudden criticizes Ashcroft's directive, claiming that it restrains Oregon doctors from easing the pain of terminally ill patients and creates a barrier to the full implementation of Oregon's law. Rudden further asserts that Oregon has put in place sufficient procedures and safeguards to prevent abuses. Rudden is director of research for the Graham Williams Group, an international public relations

Lawrence Rudden, "Death and the Law," *World & I*, vol. 18, May 2003, p. 255.
Copyright © 2003 by News World Communications, Inc. Reproduced by permission.

firm in Washington, D.C. He regularly writes articles on politics and culture.

In 1997, Oregon passed the *Death with Dignity Act*, making it the only state to permit physician-assisted suicide. Since then, the act has survived an attempt by Congress to overturn it, court hearings on its constitutional validity, and two voter initiatives, in which Oregon residents approved the measure first by a slim margin in 1994, then overwhelmingly in 1997. To qualify for assistance, patients must make two oral requests and one written request at least two weeks apart, be terminally ill with less than six months to live, and be judged mentally competent to make the decision by two separate physicians. Patients are also required to administer the medication themselves. Court records indicate that ninety-one people—mostly cancer patients—have used the provision to end their lives.

"Oregon's law is written with safeguards that prevent patients from using the law prematurely or impulsively," says George Eighmey, executive director of the Oregon branch of the Compassion in Dying Federation. According to Eighmey, patients have sought to end their lives primarily to avoid the profound loss of bodily control and dignity that often accompanies the late stages of a terminal illness.

Can the federal government deny this opportunity to spend one's final months or days in a manner that one does not consider repulsive? According to Attorney General John Ashcroft, it not only can but should. The nation's highest lawyer has declared that assisted suicide is not a "legitimate medical purpose.". . .

In November 2001, Ashcroft declared that any doctor who prescribed lethal doses of painkilling medication with the specific intent of ending his patient's life would lose his license to prescribe medications and would serve a mandatory twenty-year sentence. He defended this ultimatum on the vague grounds that doctors prescribing lethal doses of painkilling medication were in violation of the federal Controlled Substances Act (CSA), a statute intended to punish illicit trafficking of pharmaceuticals.

Supporters of the Ashcroft directive are fond of observing that it does not actually forbid doctors from helping patients end their lives. "Oregon's physicians could still practice assisted suicide, but they could not prescribe federally controlled substances for that purpose," explains Rita Marker, executive director of the International Task Force on Euthanasia and Assisted Suicide. In other words, doctors would still be free to prescribe, say, lethal doses of rat poison to Oregon's dying citizens. For obvious reasons—medical ethics, fear of lawsuits, the semblance of something resembling empathy and compassion—this will not happen. Nor, for that matter, would a doctor who had his license to prescribe drugs stripped under the Ashcroft directive be likely to remain a doctor for long. "For an oncologist to be unable to prescribe pain medication is incomprehensible," explains Oregon's Dr. Peter Rasmussen. "I would have to retire. . . . I want to continue to be a practicing physician. I would not be able to help my patients." So, despite some semantic zigzagging, the effect of the directive is really quite straightforward: to prevent states from experimenting with the practice of physician-assisted suicide. . . .

State vs. Federal Laws

Theoretically, the matter of physician-assisted suicide should be left to the states, as indicated by a 1997 Supreme Court ruling. "Throughout the nation," observed Chief Justice William Rehnquist in his majority opinion, "Americans are engaged in an earnest and profound debate about the morality, legality, and practicality of physician-assisted suicide. Our holding permits this debate to continue, as it should in a democratic society."

Having seemingly arrived at the principle that physician-assisted suicide is wrong, Ashcroft will be damned if he's going to allow the terminal patients of Oregon to exercise their legal right to end their unbearable suffering. Without so much as providing notice to Oregon officials or the general public, he has declared the practice "not medically legitimate," raising concerns that the country's top lawyer is being guided not by the nuances of law but rather by the moral certainties of personal ideology.

Of course, personal ideology is an admittedly imprecise thing, and attempts by the government to dictate what is good for the character of the nation raise a more difficult question: to whose ideology should the law adhere? Lacking a national religion or a single cultural custom, many legal issues take on a gray shade in America. Plainly, this is a good thing. History indicates that when the law and personal ideology get too close, the law often becomes a straightjacket to individual liberties. The Nazis maintained their power in part by using vague moral codes to destroy any threat to their power base. More recently, the Taliban used the law to punish all variety of sinners, from the heretics to the merely thoughtful. Early on, America's Puritan founders were also hard at work persecuting their neighbors for real and imagined shortcomings—a fact that continues to find expression in the numerous state codes regulating sexual conduct.

Though in general practice our society now tends to keep a proper distance between the law and personal ideology, this Puritan zeal for punishing what our leaders call sin may still rear its head from time to time. Exhibit A: Ashcroft's attempt to invalidate Oregon's Death with Dignity Act. Ashcroft carried the same tune while in Congress, where he twice supported legislation that would subject doctors to twenty years in prison if they prescribed federally regulated drugs to cause a patient's death. Both times the legislation failed.

Now, as attorney general, he is again insisting that physician-assisted suicide is "not a legitimate medical practice," an assessment he defends by observing that doctors are charged with helping patients live, not making them dead. Very good. Nevertheless, the Court has already allowed the administration of "risky pain relief," that is, doses of pain relief that are likely to hasten the death of a terminally ill patient. Is this procedure somehow more "legitimate" than assisted suicide? Is it medically legitimate to deny someone a right to die with dignity? Is such a right "fundamental" to patients whose condition is so severe that pain-relief medication is not sufficient to relieve their suffering? Is it somehow more medically legitimate to have politicians second-guessing doctors? And might strict federal oversight of doctors who prescribe pain medication actually have the broader effect of scaring them into undermedicating dying patients? . . .

Along the way, Ashcroft has set the stage for a classic battle of states versus federal rights. Since Oregon doctors are prescribing federally controlled medications to help Oregon residents kill themselves, the Justice Department claims jurisdiction over the process. It argues that the CSA authorizes the attorney general to revoke a practitioner's license to prescribe medications, if he determines that the practitioner is acting in a manner that "threatens public health," regardless of state laws.

Advocates of states' rights maintain that Ashcroft is expanding the scope of the CSA beyond its original intent—regulating the illegal sale of pharmaceuticals. They also dispute that he has the authority to determine whether physician-assisted suicide constitutes "a legitimate medical practice" and quiver at the idea of an unelected, unaccountable government official dictating some of the most personal decisions of their lives. This intrusion, they maintain, is a violation of the spirit of the Constitution.

Round 1 went to the states' advocates. In his harshly critical rebuke of the Ashcroft directive, Oregon federal judge Robert Jones wrote that it would be "unprecedented and extraordinary" for Congress to assign the attorney general the authority to interpret what constitutes a legitimate medical practice. While Jones acknowledged that Ashcroft may be "fully justified, morally, ethically, religiously," in opposing assisted suicide, he emphasized that the attorney general's strong feelings alone do "not permit a federal statute to be manipulated from its true meaning, even to satisfy a worthy goal."

Intrepidly, the Justice Department carries on. On September 25, 2001, it filed an appeal with the Ninth U.S. Circuit Court of Appeals—the same court that previously ruled that the due process clause of the Fourteenth Amendment prevents the government from flatly banning physician-assisted suicide. The case will be heard in spring 2003, after which an appeal to the U.S. Supreme Court is expected.[1]

Supreme Court Precedence and Individual Rights

In their 1997 ruling, the Supreme Court justices voted 9-0 that terminal patients do not have a generalized constitutional right to physician-assisted suicide. The ruling applied only to the cases before the Court and did not take into account the Oregon law. At the same time, the justices littered their opinions with enough qualifiers about specific constitutional rights and principles to effectively make a tangled mess of things. Justice Souter, for example, noted that a total ban on physician-assisted suicide could in fact be deemed unconstitutional if it violated certain basic and historically protected principles of personal autonomy. He added that there exist arguments of "increasing forcefulness for recognizing some right to a doctor's help in suicide." Justice Breyer emphasized that forcing dying patients to live out their final days in great pain might violate a general right "to die with dignity." Justice Stevens wrote a separate opinion in which he plainly stated that if presented with an appropriate case, he would overrule a ban on physician-assisted suicide. In effect, Stevens recalled

1. The court ruled in May 2004 that the federal government must authorize the use of federally controlled narcotics and other dangerous drugs that can be used to kill patients, thereby facilitating Oregon's law.

that our country does not have a national religion or culture. As our multicultural melange of citizens may have very different moral, religious, or personal ideas about how they ought to spend their final days, terminal patients should have the freedom to pursue these convictions so long as their actions affect only their own morality. In other words, an individual should not be forced to spend his final days in excruciating pain simply because this is what his neighbor feels is right. . . .

The Supreme Court emphasized that the right to physician-assisted suicide is a matter that should be decided by the states. Indeed, the democratization of this issue would have the beneficial effect of making real-world experience relevant to the law. Rather than freezing the law in accordance with the speculation of political or religious groups, we could learn from experience in a systematic fashion and thus make law adaptive to the individual needs of terminal patients.

Controls in Place in Oregon

For critics, experimentation with physician-assisted suicide would come at the unacceptable cost of making terminally ill patients vulnerable to increased pressure to end their lives—either by profit-oriented HMOs or out of implicit guilt for the financial and emotional burden they are exacting on relatives. "In an era of cost control and managed care, patients with lingering illnesses may be branded an economic liability, and decisions to encourage death can be driven by cost," says Cathy Cleaver of the U.S. Conference of Catholic Bishops. Cleaver points to the Netherlands, where physician-assisted suicide is legal and occurring at an alarming rate: "For years Dutch courts have allowed physicians to practice euthanasia and assisted suicide with impunity, supposedly only in cases where desperately ill patients have unbearable suffering. In a few years, however, Dutch policy and practice have expanded to allow the killing of people with disabilities or even physically healthy people with psychological distress; thousands of patients have been killed by their doctors without their request. The Dutch example teaches us that the 'slippery slope' is very real."

In short, Cleaver worries that if we let doctors end the pointless suffering of terminal patients, the practice would quickly become the norm. Soon depressed people would be demanding a right to die, our palliative-care options would begin to lag behind the rest of the civilized world, and our doctors would be transformed into stalking butlers. An alarming thought, but just one thing: For years the Dutch had almost no formalized procedure in place to regulate the process. Physicians were expected to report themselves to a governing board, which would determine after the fact whether they had broken the law.

By contrast, Oregon's law requires extensive reporting requirements, and, after five years, "evidence points to 100 percent reporting compliance and no deviation from the rules in Oregon," says Barbara Coombs Lee, president of the Compassion in Dying Federation. In fact, a survey of Oregon physicians who have had experience with the Death with Dignity Act reports that some candidates are being screened out of the program. According to the study, only 29 (18 percent) of the 165 people who had requested medication under the act actually received a prescription.

For those who did receive one, control over their final few days, not access to healing options, was the point. It is unlikely that critics will pause long enough to acknowledge this rousing fact. Even at this late date [2003], some of our highest government officials remain dedicated to the idea of regulating the most intimate decisions of this country's citizens, even when the outcome affects only the morality of the actor.

Truly, that is alarming.

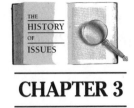

THE
HISTORY
OF
ISSUES

CHAPTER 3

The Ethical Debate

Chapter Preface

People on both sides of the debate over physician-assisted suicide claim "morality" and the "sanctity of life" as their rationale for defending their respective positions. However, they disagree on the definition of what is "moral" and what is "sacred."

Supporters of physician-assisted suicide argue it is moral to enable individuals to make the final decision in their lives—that is, choosing the time and manner of death. This argument often appeals to a secular society, one that recognizes the primacy of the individual. Ronald Dworkin, a philosopher who has provided expert counsel to the Supreme Court, says that death is "the final act of life's drama, and we want that last act to reflect our own convictions, those we have tried to live by, not the convictions of others forced on us in our vulnerable moment." Dworkin, a law professor at New York University, bases his case on the Constitution, which he says "insists that people must be free to make these deeply personal decisions for themselves and must not be forced to end their lives in a way that appalls them, just because that is what some majority thinks proper."

Opponents of euthanasia and physician-assisted suicide define what is "moral" differently. In their view, it is wrong for one human being to intentionally kill another. The Catholic Church, which remains the most formidable opponent of physician-assisted suicide, has not wavered in declaring the practice a sin against God. In his 1995 *Evangelium Vitae (Gospel of Life)*, Pope John Paul II declared assisted suicide unethical. He said, "Suicide is always as morally objectionable as murder." He maintained that for a physician to assist in a patient's suicide is "to cooperate in and at times be the actual perpetrator of an injustice that can never be excused."

The following chapter presents the various dimensions of the moral argument as espoused by both supporters and opponents of physician-assisted suicide.

Assisted Suicide Is a Transgression of Divine Sovereignty

JOHN J. PARIS AND MICHAEL P. MORELAND

In the following selection, authors John J. Paris and Michael P. Moreland declare that supporters of assisted suicide over-emphasize personal autonomy and wrongly delegate end-of-life decisions to physicians, thus violating the sovereignty of God over human life. They explain the Catholic view that human life is borrowed and that human beings do not exercise full power in living it or in ending it. The authors also analyze the 1997 Supreme Court ruling rejecting assisted suicide. They conclude that although the Court ruled against the practice, the decision was tentative and debate over an individual's right to choose when and how to die has not been settled. They add that the distinction the Court made between withdrawal of medical support, which the Catholic Church sanctions, and actively aiding suicide, which it rejects, is central to Catholic theology. Paris is a professor of bioethics in the theology department of Boston College. He has served as consultant to the President's Commission for the Study of Ethics in Medicine, the U.S. Senate Committee on Aging, and the Congressional Office of Technology Assessment. Moreland is an attorney at Williams and Connelly in Washington, D.C.

In its [1997] Ruling on physician-assisted suicide, the United States Supreme Court rejected the argument that

John J. Paris and Michael P. Moreland, *Physician Assisted Suicide: Expanding the Debate*, edited by Margaret P. Battin, Rosamond Rhodes, and Anita Silvers. New York: Routledge, 1998. Copyright © 1998 by Routledge. All rights reserved. Reproduced by permission of Routledge/Taylor & Francis Books, Inc. and the authors.

an individual's constitutionally protected "liberty interest" extends to the right to assistance in suicide. In the course of its sweeping opinions in the companion cases of *Washington v. Glucksberg* and *Vacco v. Quill* the Court noted the limited character of personal autonomy. Though we are free, we are not fully free; individuals cannot do whatever they want indifferent to the implications of their actions on themselves or on others. This concern for the well being of the individual and that of the "common good" was among the "rationally related interests" that a state may constitutionally impose on individuals' behavior. . . .

As is clear from the Court's opinion and the comments of the concurring justices, constitutional argument and legal reasoning alone have not and will not settle the debate over physician-assisted suicide. In a diverse pluralistic society there are and will continue to be widely differing values and sharply clashing choices on the issue of how we should live and when and how we should die.

Even within the unanimous Court, there was disagreement if not dissent on the role physicians should have in the death of a patient. As Justice Stevens's lengthy concurrence made obvious, those differences "are not necessarily resolved by the opinions announced today." The debate and the persuasion necessary for the enactment of policy choices remains an on-going process.

One voice in the debate on how we are to understand the meaning of life and of death is that of religion. Are we, as the Supreme Court put it in the rhetorical extravagance that marked its *Casey* [limiting state prohibition of abortion] opinion, entities who have "the right to define one's own concept of existence, of meaning, of the universe, and the mysteries of human life?" Or do we have a different and more modest role than as "masters of the universe?" If, as the Ninth Circuit [court] held in its [favorable] opinion on physician-assisted suicide, the "mastery of life" argument from *Casey* is the lodestone of our analysis, there is no and ought not be any limit on "self-sovereignty." Personal choice with regard to lifestyle as well as "how and when to die" are but corollaries of our autonomy.

Catholic View of Death

The Catholic tradition views life—and death—differently. Life is seen not as "self-creation" but as a gift of the Creator, a gift over which we are to exercise stewardship, not dominion. That stewardship demands that we be responsible for life—its protection and enhancement. We will in turn be held accountable before God not only for how we protected and developed our individual lives, but for all life. We are in the words of scripture, "Our brother's keeper."

The implication of a stewardship approach for the issue of physician-assisted suicide is, as University of Notre Dame law professor M. Cathleen Kaveny notes, that we do not have total control over our lives. Life is not ours to dispose of when we choose. It is not property which we can trade, sell, or destroy at will. In her words, "By aiming at our own deaths we usurp God's proper providence in allotting the span of our lives." In attempting to do so, we transgress what Harvard Divinity School's J. Bryan Hehir labels "the definitive limits that are entrusted to us with life—we do not own it."

Life, though, is not an end in itself. It has been given to us, as Richard McCormick, S.J., phrased it in his now-landmark 1974 *JAMA* [*Journal of the American Medical Association*] essay "To Save or Let Die," that we might achieve salvation through fidelity to the Great Commandments of love of God and love of neighbor. To achieve that goal one must enter into and be active in relationships. When the potential for those relationships is either nonexistent or exhausted, one's purpose in creation is fulfilled. When that moment is reached—in advanced old age or merely moments after birth—the duty to maintain life is ended.

McCormick elaborated on the limited duty to preserve life in a recent essay on assisted suicide:

> Life is a basic good but not an absolute one. It is basic

because, as the Congregation for the Doctrine of the Faith worded it, it is the "necessary source and condition of every human society and all of society." It is not absolute because there are higher goods for which life can be sacrificed [such as the] glory of God, salvation of souls, service of one's brethren.

Seen in this context, death is not an unmitigated evil, nor is it the enemy. Rather, it is but a stage in the pilgrimage of life. It is a hollowing out of the earthly that we might be filled and fulfilled in God. Within this understanding of life, suicide is a violation of God's dominion. It is the ultimate act of defiance—the assertion of self over divine sovereignty. . . .

The theological understanding of death as a part of the Divine Plan is the basis of the distinctions made in the Catholic moral theology between "killing and letting die"; "active and passive euthanasia"; "omission and commission"; "foreseeing and intending"; "allowing and causing." The clarity of these traditional distinctions has often been obscured. In recent years, philosophers and jurists alike have with regularity dismissed the distinction between killing and letting die as at best "a mere quibble." But as the Supreme Court has now ruled, though the distinction might at times be difficult to discern, "the two acts are widely and reasonably regarded as quite distinct."

The Price of Medical Successes

Though the role and meaning of death have been the focus of the Catholic critique of physician-assisted suicide, it is not suicide itself that is the focal point of the present policy debate. What is new in our era is the desire to medicalize suicide and active euthanasia. We want physicians to provide the means to end life in an antiseptically acceptable fashion. Knives, guns, ropes, and bridges tend to be messy. We seek a more aesthetically pleasing way of terminating life, one that leaves the patient looking dead, but not disgusting. For this, as in so much else in the twentieth-century quest for happiness, we turn to the physician.

What has led to this situation, one so fundamentally at odds with the 2500-year-old Hippocratic tradition that the physician as healer was never to administer a lethal potion? In large part, today's demands are a result of medicine's successes. We have come to believe that the "miracles" of modern medicine can not only defeat disease but conquer death. With the rise of technological medicine, lives which once were beyond rescue can now be saved. Sometimes, however, that success comes at too great a price: a life suffused in suffering, pain, and despair.

Once the quest for salvation through science and immortality through medicine proves unavailing, we seek a different medical "fix" for our problem. Since we fear death and the unrelieved suffering that prolonged dying can produce, we turn to medicine for relief from both. Commenting on that issue, Daniel Callahan writes that the movement to legalize euthanasia and assisted suicide is an "historically inevitable response to that fear." He traces that response to what Joseph Cardinal Bernardin has described as the "increasingly mechanistic, commercial, and soulless" process of modern medicine. "Caring" which traditionally characterized the profession is now being pushed aside for profit. In such an environment it is not surprising that [physician-assisted suicide crusader] Jack Kevorkian is held up as the model of a "good doctor."

Kevorkian is, in [bioethicist] George Annas's description, not simply an aberrant physician; he is "a symptom of a medical care system gone seriously wrong at the end of life." It is a system that treats death not as the Church teaches, as integral a part of nature as birth and life itself, but as "an offense against nature"—something to be fought off at all cost or, if that battle is not successful, to slay.

The inability of modern medicine to reassure us that it can manage our dying with dignity and comfort, a reality documented in the recent SUPPORT study finding that half of all conscious patients who died in the hospital experienced moderate to severe pain at least half the time during their last three days of life, leads to the demand that we be allowed to take back control of our fate. In the face of this powerful, almost relentless dynamic, Callahan asks how we accomplish that goal. He observes that "for many, the answer seems obvious and unavoidable, that of active euthanasia and assisted suicide."

The 1991 referendum in Washington state was the first public attempt to achieve that end. Though defeated in a close vote, that referendum set the stage for the successful ballot measure three years later in Oregon where, for the first time in our nation's history, voters sanctioned state approval of physician-assisted suicide. The outcome in Oregon was not surprising. Public opinion polls in this country consistently show 65 percent of the populace supporting such a proposition. In great part that support is a reflection of two cultural phenomena that have emerged and flourished over the last twenty-five years: an emphasis on individual autonomy and the transformation of American medicine from a caring profession into a business designed to serve demands for medical services.

One of the striking features of this shift was the triumph of the patient "rights" movement over and against the long-standing tradition of medical paternalism. The corollary of the emphasis on patient autonomy was the obligation of medicine to respond to patient desires. The legislative response to that emphasis was the Patient Self-Determination Act [PSDA] of 1990 in which Congress mandated that healthcare facilities must inform patients of their right to decline any unwanted medical treatment, including those that were potentially life-prolonging.

Important Distinctions

In enacting the PSDA, the Congress was implicitly following four hundred years of consistent Catholic moral teaching that no one is obliged to undergo a proposed medical treatment that is disproportionately painful or burdensome. That doctrine is best summed up in the Vatican's

1980 *Declaration on Euthanasia*, where we read:

> One cannot impose on anyone the obligation to have recourse to a technique which is already in use but which carries a risk or is burdensome. Such a refusal is not the equivalent of suicide (or euthanasia); on the contrary, it should be considered as an acceptance of the human condition, or a wish to avoid the application of a medical procedure disproportionate to the results that can be expected.

That *Declaration*, however, makes a sharp distinction between refusing measures that would serve "only [to sustain] a precarious and burdensome prolongation of life" and suicide or active euthanasia. The former is permitted; the latter is prohibited.

The word euthanasia ("a good death") is subject to widely differing understandings, and the distinction between active and passive euthanasia (killing and letting die) is, as we have seen in the appellate court rulings, frequently collapsed into the one term. James Rachels' now famous 1975 *New England Journal of Medicine* essay on "Active and Passive Euthanasia" was the first to deny that there is any real difference between the two. For him, "if a doctor lets a patient die, for humane reasons, he is in the same moral position as if he had given the patient a lethal injection."

The supporters of unlimited patient autonomy agree. They place no constraint and no limitation on an individual's autonomous "right" to direct medical treatment. The patient alone determines not only what medical intervention will be undergone, but whether medicine should be enlisted in the ending of life itself. As the highly publicized [1997] Philosophers' Brief to the Supreme Court in the physician-assisted suicide case starkly puts it:

> If it is permissible for a doctor deliberately to withdraw medical treatment in order to allow death to result from a natural process, then it is equally permissible for him to help a patient hasten his own death more actively, if that is the patient's express wish.

That brief, as does the ruling of the Second Circuit Court of Appeals in *Quill*, rejects any distinction between killing and letting die. As Ronald Dworkin, the principal author of the Philosophers' Brief, noted in a commentary on the oral argument before the Supreme Court in the physician-assisted suicide cases:

> One justice suggested that a patient who insists that life support be disconnected is not committing suicide. That's wrong: he is committing suicide if he aims at death, as most such patients do. Just as someone whose wrist is cut in an accident is committing suicide if he refuses to try to stop the bleeding.

If that thesis is correct, we land in one of two seemingly untenable positions:

1. If killing is seen as morally wrong, then we cannot withdraw life-prolonging medical procedures that are overly burdensome to the patient. That was the argument made by the trial court in the *Quinlan* case when Judge Robert Muir ruled that removing the ventilator would subject the physicians to charges of homicide. Such rulings, which allow "no exit" from medical technology, are characterized by Daniel Callahan as "a clear case of slavery to technology." They also lead to cries for relief, including demands for active euthanasia.

2. Alternatively, if there is no distinction between killing and letting die and one holds, as do all of the courts of final jurisdiction that have addressed the issue, that it is morally and legally acceptable to withhold or withdraw unwanted medical interventions, then there is no barrier to "killing" the patient. As Rachels puts it, the physician is in the same moral position "if he [gives] the patient a lethal injection as in withdrawing a respirator." In fact, Rachels argued [that] since the latter action spares the patient from suffering, it is "actually preferable."

To avoid confusion in this debate, it is imperative to have a clear definition of terms. Here euthanasia is defined as the deliberate action by a physician to terminate the life of a patient. The clearest example is the act of lethal injection. Singer and Siegler's 1991 *New England Journal of Medicine* essay on "Euthanasia—A Critique" provides the helpful distinction between that action and such other acts as the decision to forego life-sustaining treatment (including the use of ventilations, cardio-pulmonary resuscitation, dialysis, or tube feedings); or the administration of analgesic agents to relieve pain; or "assisted suicide" in which the doctor prescribes but does not administer a lethal dose of medication; or "mercy killing" performed by a patient's family or friends.

Catholic Opposition to Intentional Killing

Catholic tradition, as the Vatican *Declaration* makes clear, opposes euthanasia or the direct intentional killing of innocent life, whether of "a fetus or an embryo, an infant or an adult, an old person, or one suffering from an incurable disease, or a person who is dying." Furthermore, the Church holds that "no one is permitted to ask for this act of killing for himself or herself," nor is it morally licit to consent to such an action for one entrusted to your care. The reason for these moral imperatives is found in the *Declaration's* statement: "Only the Creator of life has the right to take away the life of the innocent." To arrogate that right to ourselves, whether as patient, guardian, or caregiver would be a "violation of the divine law" and "an offense against the dignity of the human person."

Referenda, legislative enactments, or judicial approval of state-sanctioned physician assistance in death stand as a challenge to that tradition. What is being asked for in these movements is most clearly seen in the Washington state referendum where voters were asked to approve what its proponents labeled "a new medical service": authorization for physicians actively to assist a terminally ill patient to die.

The ballot initiative was circulated with the title, "Shall adult patients who are in a medically terminal condition be permitted to request and receive from a physician aid-in-dying?" Beneath that innocuously worded heading was the reality that "aid-in-dying" meant "aid in the form of a medical service, provided in person by a physician, that will end the life of a conscious and mentally qualified patient in a dignified, painless, and humane manner, when requested voluntarily by the patient through a written directive . . . at the time the medical service is to be provided."

Overemphasis on Autonomy

From the time of [Greek physician] Hippocrates through the 1997 *Current Opinions* of the Council on Ethical and Judicial Affairs of the American Medical Association, Western medicine has regarded the killing of patients, even on request, as a profound violation of the deepest meaning of the medical vocation. [Bioethicist] Leon Kass undertook to explain the reasons for the societal change on this question in a probing essay in *The Public Interest* entitled "Why Doctors Must Not Kill." There he argued that the basis for the shift in attitude, which has already led to some 5,000 cases of active euthanasia or assisted suicide a year in the Netherlands, is an overemphasis on freedom and personal autonomy, expressed in the view that each one has a right to control his or her body and life, including the end of it. In this view, physicians are bound to acquiesce not only to demands for termination of treatment, but also to intentional killing through poison, because the right to choose—freedom—must be respected even more than life itself. The second reason advanced for killing patients is not a concern for choice but the assessment by the patient or others that the patient's life is no longer deemed worth living. It is not autonomy but the miserable or pitiable condition of the body or mind that warrants, in Kass's words, "doing the patient in."

Both of these positions, individual autonomy and a life

so devoid of dignity it should be destroyed, run counter to the Catholic understanding of life as a divine gift over which we exercise stewardship not dominion. Rather than the complete control over life demanded by the Philosophers' Brief in which life is to be ended when we conclude that living on "would disfigure rather than enhance the lives we have created," the Christian finds death's meaning in the example of the suffering Savior who abandoned himself in perfect obedience to the Father's will.

The recent example of Joseph Cardinal Bernardin's very public dying, which *Newsweek* captured in a cover story as "Teaching Us How to Die," stands in sharp contrast to the view that control and domination over death should be our goal. As Bernardin expressed it in his parting legacy, *The Gift of Peace*, "I now realize that when I asked my doctor for the test results [of his metastatic cancer], I had to let go of everything. God was teaching me how little control we really have." Bernardin's conclusion when he understood that he was dying was uncomplicated: "[God] is now calling me home."

Self-abandonment to the will of God, not self-determination or the triumph of the human will, is the Christian response when medicine is unable to reverse the dying process. This is because in the Christian tradition death is not the final victor; it is, rather, a "transition from earthy life to life eternal."

Assisted Suicide Does Not Violate the Sanctity of Life

JOHN SHELBY SPONG

In the following article, John Shelby Spong, a prominent leader of the Episcopal Church, argues that assisted suicide should be allowed under restricted circumstances. Spong believes that once individuals lose the capacity to interact meaningfully with other people and God, they should be allowed to die. He explains that in the past, when medical care was rudimentary and death seemed to be entirely in the hands of God, the issue of euthanasia was simpler. Humans had little technology that could prolong life. In modern times, however, science endows doctors with previously unimagined powers to keep a body alive even when that person no longer has any quality of life. Spong believes that assisting in such a person's suicide does not violate the sanctity of life. However, to prevent people from being victimized by family members who could profit from the death of a relative, safeguards need to be established. These include requiring people to have living wills specifying the extent of treatment they want in the event of a serious accident or illness and requiring hospitals to have a bioethics committee to help decide on issues of euthanasia. At the time of writing, Spong was bishop of the Episcopal Diocese of Newark, New Jersey. A prodigious writer and lecturer, he is the author of numerous books, including Liberating the Gospels: Reading the Bible with Jewish Eyes, Why Chris-

John Shelby Spong, "In Defense of Assisted Suicide," *The Human Quest*, vol. 210, no. 3, May/June 1996, pp. 11–12. Copyright © 1996 by *The Human Quest*. Reproduced by permission of the author.

tianity Must Change or Die: A Bishop Speaks to Believers in Exile, *and* The Bishops' Voice. *Retiring as bishop of Newark in 2000, he currently serves on the House of Bishops' Theology Committee of the Episcopal Church.*

What gives life its value? What gives life its meaning? If value and meaning are removed from life before life ceases to exist, is it then still life? Do potential value and potential meaning attach themselves to fetal life that is so embryonic as to be only potential, not actual? Who has the right to make decisions about life that is only potential? Is it the society? Is it the affected individuals or the bearer of that life? Does the sacredness ascribed by religious systems through the ages to human life reside in our biological processes? Is biological life itself sacred whether it be human or otherwise?

It is around these questions that debates swirl in [the twentieth century] on such ethical issues as euthanasia, assisted suicide, birth control, abortion, animal rights, the use of animal organs and parts in human attempts to combat diseases, vegetarianism and many environmental concerns. In most of these debates the emotional content is high. The person operates on the basis of an unstated but assumed answer to these questions that is passionately held. Frequently that answer is so deeply related to the core of the person's being that it allows no opposition. So the result is argument, not dialogue, and heat, not light.

One of these issues is today coming before our society with increasing rapidity and it requires of the Christian Church a response. Is active, as well as passive, euthanasia an acceptable practice within the ethics of Christian people? To state it more boldly, is assisted suicide an ethical option for Christians and, if so, under what circumstances?. . .

The first thing that must be noted is that these issues are peculiarly modern ones. A century ago and, in most cases, even fifty years ago, these issues would hardly ever have arisen. Throughout western history, society in general, and the medical profession in particular, has been passionately dedicated to the preservation of life. The assumption commonly held was that life was sacred, that it bore the image of God and that its limits had been set by God. So deep was this conviction in the Judeo/Christian world, that murder was not only prohibited among members of the same tribe, but it was also surrounded by powerful disincentives.

In the biblical code, when murder occurred, blood retribution was the legal right and moral duty of the victim's nearest of kin. To escape immediate vengeance and to determine whether or not extenuating circumstances existed, cities of refuge were set up for those who accidentally killed a fellow Jew. In these centers the killer could find temporary sanctuary until the case could be decided and the verdict rendered by the society. If the murder was in fact accidental, then innocence and freedom was established. But if not, then guilt and the delivery of the killer to the family of the victim could be pronounced.

Of course the killing of an enemy was not covered by this prohibition. Thus the Hebrew scriptures had no conflict in proclaiming that the same God who said. "You shall not kill" as part of the Ten Commandments could also order Saul to slay every "man, woman, infant and suckling," among the Amalekites (I Sam. 15:3). Even suicide was rare indeed in this religious tradition, so deep was this sense of the sacredness of life.

Modern Technology Has Changed Experience

But in that world surgery was limited to the sawing off of a limb. Antibiotics were unknown. Blood transfusions could not be given. Organ transplants were inconceivable. Intravenous feeding was unheard of. Finally, machines or medicines that could stimulate the heart and lungs could not be imagined. The time of death did seem to be in the hands of God. Human skill could do little to prolong it. So the idea grew and became deeply rooted in the pysche of the whole society that the sole task of medical science was to prolong life. That was a noble value then and it remains so today.

The realities of our world, however, have changed dramatically. That which was inconceivable, unimaginable and unheard of is now a part of our contemporary experience. We have extended the boundaries of life to where the values and definitions of yesterday collide with the technology and skill of today. That is why the debate on assisted suicide now looms before us and that is why this generation must question the conclusions of the past.

Let me pose the complexities of this issue by asking a series of questions. In what does the sanctity of life reside? Is life sacred when pain is intense and incurable? Is it a value to drug a patient into insensibility for pain while continuing to keep him or her alive biologically? At what point does the quality of life outweigh the value found in the quantity of life? Is life's meaning found in the physical activities of the body or in the relationships that interact with the person whose physical body is alive? If those relationships can no longer exist, should the body be allowed to continue functioning? Who should make the life and death decisions in this world? Should that power be given to doctors? But doctors today are less and less involved with patients as medicine becomes more and more impersonal and complex.

Ethical Questions

Since doctors still profit from hospital visits to their patients, we must recognize that there is a financial incentive to doctors to keep lingering patients alive. Should this decision be left to the family members? But there are cases in which family members have profited from the death of a relative. Family members have been known to kill a parent or a spouse when they had a vested interest in that person's demise. Should that decision then be left to chaplains, rabbis, pastors or priests? But the religious institutions today are too weak to carry such a responsibility, since perhaps half of the population of our nation is today not related to any religious institution. It might also need to be said that even members of this professional group of "God bearers" have not always been strangers to self-serving corruption. Can the decision be left to the individual involved? Certainly that person needs to be involved in that decision if at all possible, but can it be solely the decision of one person? Should extraordinary care for terminally ill persons be allowed to bankrupt families? Where is the point where such care becomes destructive to the economic well being of the remaining family members? Because this generation is now capable of certain procedures, is there some moral necessity to use those procedures?

Given the interdependence today of the health of the whole society through insurance rates, Medicare and Medicaid, extraordinary measures to prolong life universally applied would bankrupt the whole nation. Already this nation spends more than 80 cents of every health care dollar in the last year of the person's life. Should such life supports then be available only to those who can afford them? Would we then be equating the sacredness of life and the values that grow out of that concept with wealth? If health care has to be rationed, as it increasingly is in the managed care contracts, on what basis are extraordinary procedures to be withheld?

The Debate Must Be Engaged

The values of yesterday are colliding with the technological and medical expertise of today, rendering the conclusions of the past inoperative for the future. That is why questions abound and debate rages around the issues of life and death at both ends of life's spectrum. Even the word "murder" is being redefined in this debate. Is a doctor who performs an abortion a murderer? Is Dr. Jack Kevorkian [physician-assisted suicide crusader] a murderer? Should he be prosecuted for assisting people into death when hope for those persons had expired? Is it murder for a father who can no longer bear to see his child in intense pain or lingering malaise when all conscious function has been lost, to take matters into his own hands? Is it murder for a wife of long years to order no further food to be given to her dying husband in order to speed his death? Would it be different if she placed a plastic bag over his head? Would one be more moral than the other?

The lines are so vague, the decisions so awesome, the fear so great, the values of the past so compromised by the technology of today, that by not facing these issues consciously society will drift into decisions by default and a new uncritical consensus will become normative. The debate must be engaged and Christians must be part of it.

I, for one, am no longer willing to be silent on this issue. I, as a Christian, want to state publicly my present conclusions. After much internal wrestling, I can now say with conviction that I favor both active and passive euthanasia, and I also believe that assisted suicide should be legalized, but only under circumstances that would effectively preclude both self-interest and malevolence.

Perhaps a place to start would be to require by law that living wills be mandatory for all people. A second step might be to require every hospital and every community to have a bioethics committee, made up of the most respected leadership people available, to which a patient, family members, doctors or clergy persons could appeal for objective help in making these rending decisions.

My conclusions are based on the conviction that the sacredness of my life is not ultimately found in my biological extension. It is found rather in the touch, the smile and the love of those to whom I can knowingly respond. When that ability to respond disappears permanently, so, I believe, does the meaning and the value of my biological life. Even my hope of life beyond biological death is vested in a living relationship with the God who, my faith tradition teaches me, calls me by name. I believe that the image of God is formed in me by my ability to respond to that calling Deity. If that is so, then the image of God has moved beyond my mortal body when my ability to respond consciously to that Divine Presence disappears. So nothing sacred is compromised by assisting my death in those circumstances.

So into these issues Christian people must venture. It is a terrain fraught with fear and subject to demagoguery by the frightened religious right. That is why the mainline churches must consider these issues in the public arena where faith, knowledge, learning and tradition can blend to produce understanding.

Legalized Euthanasia in the Netherlands Has Resulted in Many Deaths Without Consent

HERBERT HENDIN

In this article, Herbert Hendin asserts that legalizing euthanasia is dangerous because guidelines restricting the practice are easily abused, leading to the killing of people without their consent. He supports his case by citing two studies on euthanasia in the Netherlands, which enacted a statute in 1993 that protects physicians practicing euthanasia if they follow strict guidelines. The author disagrees with the Dutch claim that allowing the practice of euthanasia for dying patients has not led to the so-called slippery slope, the extension of assisted suicide to individuals who are not terminally ill. According to a 1990 study, physicians ended the lives of 1,030 people without consulting them. A 1995 study indicates that 948 patients were euthanized without their consent. Hendin is a professor of psychiatry and behavioral sciences at New York Medical College and the medical director of the American Foundation for Suicide Prevention. His publications

Herbert Hendin, *The Case Against Assisted Suicide: For the Right to End-of-Life Care*, edited by Kathleen Foley and Herbert Hendin. Baltimore, MD: The Johns Hopkins University Press, 2002. Copyright © 2002 by The Johns Hopkins University Press. All rights reserved. Reproduced by permission.

include Suicide in America; Seduced by Death: Doctors, Patients, and the Dutch Cure; *and* The Case Against Assisted Suicide: For the Right to End-of-Life Care *(with Kathleen Foley). Hendin has provided expert advice on euthanasia and assisted suicide to the U.S. House of Representatives Committee on the Judiciary.*

In the spring of 2001 the Dutch Parliament passed a statute that formally legalized euthanasia and physician-assisted suicide in the Netherlands. Although the world media treated the passage as a major event, both practices had long been legally sanctioned as the result of a series of case decisions going back to the early 1970s that had made the Netherlands the only country where euthanasia and physician-assisted suicide were widely practiced.

Those in the Netherlands who seek an explanation for the Dutch embrace of assisted suicide and euthanasia usually emphasize the country's historical tradition of tolerance. The Dutch had fought to secure their religious freedom in the sixteenth and seventeenth centuries, and the Netherlands became a refuge for Jews, Catholics, and free thinkers like [Spanish philosopher Benedict] Spinoza and [French philosopher René] Descartes who fled there from religious oppression. Dutch secular society in the same period was marked by the Netherlands becoming a major maritime power whose merchants had to learn to accept different cultures, traditions, and practices. . . .

In 1973, against a background of social ferment, a euthanasia case first received widespread public attention in the Netherlands: a physician ended the life of her ailing seventy-eight-year-old mother at her mother's request. Popular support grew for the physician and for the Dutch court in Leeuwarden that found her guilty but refused to punish her. The court relied on an expert witness, a medical inspector for the national health service, who stated that it was no longer considered right for physicians to keep patients alive to the bitter end under certain conditions. These conditions were spelled out in detail in a subsequent case when, in 1981, a Rotterdam court, in finding a layperson guilty of assisting in a suicide, volunteered the opinion that a physician doing so might be exempt from punishment under the Dutch penal code if there had been a voluntary request from a person suffering unbearably with no reasonable alternatives for relief and if the physician had consulted with another physician in making the decision.

In 1984, a case reached the Dutch Supreme Court. A physician who had assisted in the suicide of a ninety-five-year-old woman had been acquitted, but the decision for acquittal was reversed by an appellate court. The Supreme Court overturned the conviction, arguing that the appellate court had failed to consider whether the physician was placed in an intolerable position because of what it called a "conflict of duties." Was the patient's suffering such that the physician was forced to act in a situation "beyond [his or her] control?" The court referred the case back to an appellate court in The Hague [The Netherlands' capital] with the instruction to consider the case with one dominant consideration from an objective medical perspective: could the euthanasia practiced by the physician be regarded as an action justified in a situation of medical necessity?

Prosecutions Were Rare

This ruling invited and obliged the prosecutor in The Hague to rely heavily on the opinion of the Royal Dutch Medical Association (KNMG) as to the acceptability of euthanasia from the professions' standpoint. Critics of the Supreme Court's ruling were unhappy at what they perceived as the court's abdication of moral and legal authority to the medical profession. The statement given by the KNMG to the appellate court paraphrased the Supreme Court's language to declare that in a situation of necessity (force majeure) a physician could be justified in honoring a request for euthanasia.

Even before the decision was issued in The Hague dismissing the charges against the physician, the KNMG had sent a letter to the Minister of Justice asking for a change in the law to permit euthanasia. Although there was public sympathy for the physicians involved in the euthanasia cases and support for the practice of euthanasia, there was not then support for changing the statute. Physicians were able to practice euthanasia with only the protection of case law. Prosecutions, however, were rare, and punishment, even in cases of conviction, was virtually nonexistent.

Eventually, a consensus on guidelines for practicing euthanasia was reached by the courts, the KNMG, the Ministry of Justice, and the Dutch Health Council. When patients experiencing intolerable suffering that could not be relieved in any other way made a voluntary, well-considered, and persistent request to a physician for euthanasia, the physician, if supported in the decision by another physician, would be justified in performing euthanasia. The doctor should not certify the death as due to natural causes and should notify the medical examiner, who would file a report with the local prosecutor, who could investigate further or allow the deceased to be buried. If these guidelines were followed the physician would not be prosecuted under Dutch law that, at the time, treated euthanasia as a criminal offense. In 1993, a statute was enacted that gave further protection to physicians by explicitly stipulating that a physician following the guidelines would not be prosecuted.

In response to domestic and international concern about reports of abuse, the Dutch government sponsored a study of physician-assisted suicide and euthanasia in 1990. That study, which was largely replicated in a 1995 study, was supported by the KNMG with the promise that physicians who participated would receive immunity from prosecution for anything they revealed.

In 1996 the investigators published a report of their new findings in Dutch and summarized their work in two articles in the *New England Journal of Medicine* which were supported by an editorial in that journal. These reports concluded that, since matters had not grown worse during the five years between the two studies, there was no evidence that "physicians in the Netherlands are moving down a slippery slope." In this context, the "slippery slope" is the gradual extension of assisted suicide to widening groups of patients after it is legally permitted for patients designated as terminally ill. . . .

Results of 1990 and 1995 Studies

Comparing the data for the 1990 and 1995 studies is revealing. From 1990 to 1995, the death rate from euthanasia increased from 1.9 percent to 2.2 percent of all deaths, when based on interviews with 405 Dutch physicians selected from a stratified random sample. The rate increased from 1.7 percent to 2.4 percent when based on responses to a questionnaire completed by more than 4,600 physicians in both years. The increase in euthanasia deaths, ranging from 16 percent to 41 percent (from 573 to 1,064 deaths), would seem significant, but the *Dutch* investigators do not regard it as such even though they give "generational and cultural changes in patients' attitudes" as a possible explanation for the increase. The investigators describe the rates of physician-assisted suicide as remaining constant and low although, based on the interview study, the actual number increased from 380 to 542.

Guidelines Have Failed

The extension of euthanasia to more patients has been associated with the inability to regulate the process within established rules. Virtually every guideline set up by the Dutch—a voluntary, well-considered, persistent request; intolerable suffering that cannot be relieved; formal consultation with a colleague; and reporting of cases—has failed to protect patients or has been modified or violated.

Many of the violations are evident from the officially sanctioned studies. For example, the studies reveal that more than 50 percent of physicians considered it appropriate to suggest euthanasia to patients. Neither the physicians nor the study's investigators seem to acknowledge how much the voluntariness of the process may be compromised by such a suggestion.

Intolerable suffering that cannot be relieved has always been regarded as a necessary criterion for euthanasia in the Netherlands. In 74 percent of cases, physicians reported that such suffering was the major reason for patients requesting euthanasia. In a quarter of cases, however, fear of future suffering or loss of dignity was more important; neither of these reasons by itself would seem to satisfy the criterion of unrelievable suffering.

What if patients do not want treatments that will relieve their suffering? That is their right in the Netherlands as elsewhere, but then they do not meet the criterion for euthanasia. The Dutch Supreme Court affirmed that with regard to mental suffering, euthanasia is not permissible if palliative treatment is possible, even if it is refused by the patient. The KNMG stated that this should be true for somatically based suffering as well. In 17 percent of cases in 1995, however, physicians admitted that even though treatment alternatives had been available, euthanasia was performed.

Consultation takes place in about 80 percent of the reported cases, but interviews with physicians revealed that in only 11 percent of the unreported cases was there consultation with another physician. Taken together, these figures indicate that there is consultation in about half of Dutch euthanasia cases. When life was terminated without request, there was no consultation in 97 percent of cases.

Of the physicians who had been a consultant more than once, 50 percent had previously been consulted by the same physician; 24 percent had themselves previously consulted the attending physician in euthanasia cases of their own. Recognizing that such "pairs" may compromise the independence of consultants, the Dutch investigators subsequently recommended that independent consultants be chosen. In the overwhelming majority of cases, the physician's mind had been made up before consulting; not surprisingly, the consulting doctor disagreed in only 7 percent of cases. In 12 percent of cases the consulting physician did not actually see the patient. Convenience of location and agreement on life-ending decisions were the major reasons given for consulting a particular physician; knowledge of palliative care was hardly mentioned.

Under-reporting has been a serious problem. In only 18 percent of cases in 1990 had physicians reported their euthanasia cases to the authorities as required by Dutch guidelines. To encourage more reporting of cases, a simplified notification procedure was enacted. It ensured that physicians would not be prosecuted if guidelines were followed. The investigators credit this procedural change with contributing to an increase in the cases reported to 41 percent by 1995, while acknowledging that a 59 percent rate of unreported cases is still disturbingly high.

The Dutch studies reveal that half of the physicians who had not reported their most recent case of euthanasia gave as a reason their wish or that of their family to avoid a judicial inquiry, 20 percent the fear of prosecution, 16 percent the failure to fulfill the requirements for accepted procedures, and 14 percent the belief that euthanasia should be a private matter. Between 15 percent and 20 percent of doctors say they will not report their cases under any circumstances. Twenty percent of the physicians' most recent unreported cases involved ending a life without the patient's consent. Such cases, both the 1990 and 1995 studies revealed, were virtually never reported.

Death Without Consent

The most alarming concern to arise from the Dutch studies has been the documentation of cases in which patients who have not given their consent have had their lives ended by physicians. The 1990 study revealed that in 0.8 percent of the deaths (more than 1,000 cases) in the

Netherlands each year, physicians admitted they actively caused death without the explicit consent of the patient. The 1995 figure is 0.7 percent (fewer than 1,000 cases), but the researchers, while pointing to the decline, concede that differences in the way this particular information was obtained make its significance uncertain. In both studies, however, about a quarter of physicians stated that they had "terminated the lives of patients without explicit request" from the patient to do so, and a third more of the physicians could conceive of doing so. The use of the word *explicit* is somewhat inaccurate, since in 48 percent of these cases there was no request of any kind and in the others there were mainly references to patients' earlier statements of not wanting to suffer.

The 1990 study documented, and the 1995 study confirmed, that cases classified as "termination of the patient without explicit request" were a fraction of the nonvoluntary and involuntary euthanasia cases. International attention had centered on the 1,350 cases (1% of all Dutch deaths) in 1990 in which physicians gave pain medication with the explicit intention of ending the patient's life. The investigators minimized the number of patients put to death who had not requested it by not including these 1,350 patients in that category.

By 1995 there had been an increase in the number of deaths in which physicians gave pain medication with the explicit intention of ending the patient's life from 1,350 cases to 1,896 (1.4% of all Dutch deaths). These are comparisons that the Dutch investigators do not make. As reported by the physicians in the 1995 study, in more than 80 percent of these cases (1,537 deaths), no request for death was made by the patient. Since these are cases of nonvoluntary, and involuntary (if the patient was competent), euthanasia, this is a striking increase in the number of lives terminated without request and a refutation of the investigators' claim that there has been perhaps a slight decrease in the number of such cases.

If one totals all the deaths that resulted from euthanasia, assisted suicide, ending the life of a patient without consent, and giving opioids with the explicit intention of ending life, the estimated number of deaths caused by active intervention by physicians increased from 4,813 (3.7% of all deaths) in 1990 to 6,368 (4.7% of all deaths) in 1995. Based on data from the questionnaire study, this is an increase of 27 percent in cases in which physicians actively intervened to cause death. Of the more than 6,000 deaths in which physicians admit to having actively and intentionally intervened to cause death, 40 percent involved no explicit request from the patient for them to do so.

The Dutch investigators minimize the significance of the number of deaths without consent by explaining that the patients were incompetent. But in the 1995 study, 21 percent of the individuals classified as "patients whose lives were ended without explicit request" were competent; in the 1990 study, 37 percent were competent. We are not told what percentage of those patients who were given pain medication intended to end their lives without discussing it with them were competent, but analysis of the data for opioid administration indicated that it is likely to be at least 20 percent.

More than 4,000 additional competent patients were given pain medication in amounts likely to end their lives by physicians who did not discuss the decision with them, but whose primary intention was not to end their lives. Whether the intention was to end life or whether death was simply likely, physicians usually gave as the reason for not discussing the decisions with the patients that they had previously had some discussion of the subject with the patients. Apparently they thought that was sufficient justification for ending a life or putting it at risk without determining the patient's current wishes. . . .

Procedure, Not Substance

Consistent with its view that any Dutch problems with euthanasia are basically procedural, the KNMG has made various recommendations to improve the procedures for dealing with euthanasia cases without addressing the basic substantive problems. In 1995 the organization refined its guidelines: assisted suicide rather than euthanasia should be performed whenever possible; a second physician who has no professional or personal ties to the first should actually see the patient; physicians need not participate in euthanasia but must refer the patient to doctors who will; and physicians must report all cases of euthanasia to the authorities.

The protection of the patient is usually cited as the reason for preferring assisted suicide to euthanasia, but the strain on the doctor was given by the KNMG as the reason for this suggested change. A KNMG spokesperson explained that "many doctors find euthanasia a difficult and burdensome action and the patient's participation diminishes the burden slightly." Physicians who perform euthanasia infrequently may follow the KNMG suggestion, and the guideline seems intended to encourage reluctant doctors to participate. Physicians who perform euthanasia more often are not likely to be deterred, since they see assisted suicide as more open to complications and failure.

The KNMG does not see a contradiction between saying that doctors need not participate in euthanasia and demanding that they make a referral that is against their conscience. The KNMG spokesperson explained that a doctor cannot "leave a patient in the cold at the last moment. He should help find alternatives." But no alternatives other than suffering or euthanasia are envisioned.

The reasonable recommendation by the KNMG that independent consultants should actually see the patients is, unfortunately, not likely to make much of a difference. Practitioners of euthanasia are known by reputation to every doctor, but they are not expert in palliative care; their seeing the patient or their not being a friend of the referring physician is not apt to change the result.

The Dutch investigators have recommended that some

physicians specialize as euthanasia consultants, building up experience in the "medico-technical aspects of assisted suicide and euthanasia and the possibilities of palliative care." Acting as a consultant in euthanasia cases, however, does not somehow make a physician knowledgeable about palliative care. My own experience with a few physicians in the Netherlands who had performed or been consultants in dozens of euthanasia cases was that they were surprisingly uninvolved in palliative care. Nor did they show sensitivity to the ambivalence that accompanies most requests to die, which was clearly evident in some of the cases we discussed. They seemed to be facilitators of the process rather than independent evaluators of the patient's situation who might be able to relieve suffering so that euthanasia seemed less necessary to the patient. One prominent consultant described his role as easing the doubts of physicians who were uncertain as to whether to go forward with euthanasia. He and the other consultants were certainly knowledgeable in the "medico-technical" aspects of euthanasia (i.e., they could end life quickly and efficiently). . . .

It is worth noting that the Dutch authors of the 1995 study concluded their report by saying that it would be desirable to reduce the number of cases in which life is terminated without the patient's request, but this must be the common responsibility of the doctor and the patient. The person who does not wish to have his or her life terminated should declare this clearly, in advance, orally and in writing, preferably in the form of a living will. In a press conference, one of the investigators went even further in stating that the person responsible for avoiding involuntary termination of life is the patient. That remark is both a harbinger of the direction in which Dutch euthanasia policies are heading and a summation of much that is wrong with them.

Dutch efforts at regulating assisted suicide and euthanasia have served as a model for proposed statutes in the United States and other countries. Yet the Dutch experience has indicated that these practices defy adequate regulation. Given legal sanction, euthanasia, intended originally for the exceptional case, has become an accepted way of dealing with serious or terminal illness in the Netherlands. In the process, palliative care is one of the casualties, while hospice care lags behind that of other countries.

In recent testimony before the the British House of Lords, Zbigniew Zylicz, one of the few palliative care experts practicing in the Netherlands, emphasized Dutch deficiencies in palliative care and the lack of hospice care in the Netherlands, attributing them to the availability of the easier alternative of euthanasia. In its 1997 ruling denying a constitutional right to assisted suicide, the U.S. Supreme Court cited these deficiencies in particular and the Dutch experience in general as evidence that it is dangerous to give legal sanction to assisted suicide.

Physician-Assisted Suicide Is Morally Justified

KENNETH CAUTHEN

Kenneth Cauthen is a retired professor of theology and a Baptist minister. The following selection is excerpted from his book The Ethics of Assisted Death: When Life Becomes a Burden Too Hard to Bear. *In it, Cauthen maintains that when a patient's pain and suffering have become unbearable, it is ethical for a physician to help that patient die. Patients in this situation have the right to make the choice to die, he insists. Moreover, it is the duty of physicians to do what is best for those who are under their care, and sometimes this means assisting them to hasten death.*

Deciding what is right is especially difficult when the permissibility of deliberately ending a human life is involved. In these extreme situations the normal rules of morality are stretched to the breaking point. Self-defense against a would-be murderer, killing enemy soldiers in war, capital punishment for the most horrendous crimes, intentional suicide by a spy to prevent torture or a coerced disclosure of vital military information, killing a berserk man who is systematically murdering a line of hostages— all these instances pose questions that severely test our moral wisdom.

Nearly everyone would agree that in some of the cases

Kenneth Cauthen, *The Ethics of Assisted Death: When Life Becomes a Burden Too Hard to Bear.* Lima, OH: CSS Publishing Company, 1999. Copyright © 1999 by CSS Publishing Company, PO Box 4503, Lima, OH 45802-4503. Reproduced by permission.

listed it would be legitimate to end a life deliberately. This fact tells us that killing a person is not always and necessarily regarded as wrong. It all depends upon the circumstances. Now enters the question of physician-assisted death.

I want to make a cautious argument that under some carefully limited circumstances, it is permissible for a physician to assist a person [to] hasten death to end unwanted, intolerable, unnecessary suffering. This includes providing medicines or other means the patient can use to commit suicide or by directly administering medicines that end the patient's life.

Patient Choice

1. *In some situations the choice of the patient takes priority over other considerations.* Consider a person with an incurable illness or severe debility such that life has become so racked with pain or so burdensome that desirable, meaningful, purposeful existence has ceased. Suppose that person says, "My life is no longer worth living; I cannot stand it any longer; I want to end it now to avoid further pain, indignity, torment, and despair." In the end after all alternatives have been thoroughly considered, I believe this person has the right to make a choice to die and that it ought to be honored. We would want to urge consultation with physicians, clergy, lawyers, therapists, family, and others so that such a serious and irreversible decision can be made after sufficient time has passed and every alternative thoroughly weighed. We have obligations to others and should take their needs into account. The state has an interest in protecting life. But, in the end, individuals should be given wide latitude in deciding when life has become an unendurable hardship.

2. *The role of the physician is to do what is best for the patient, and in some extreme situations this may include hastening death upon the voluntary request of the dying.* Many doctors protest that they are committed to preserve and

enhance life, not to end it deliberately. If the role of the physician is defined solely in terms of healing, then, of course, this excludes assisting someone to die. This is the wrong way to go about defining the scope and limits of the doctor's proper function. I suggest that the question should be put this way: What is the best thing I can do to help my patients in whatever circumstances arise, given my special knowledge and skills? In nearly every case the answer will be to heal, to prolong life, to reduce suffering, to restore health and physical well-being, i.e., to preserve and enhance life. But in some extreme, hopeless circumstances, the best service a physician can render may be to help a person hasten death in order to relieve intolerable, unnecessary suffering that makes life unbearable as judged by the patient. This would be an enlargement of the physician's role, not a contradiction of it.

Ending Suffering

3. *Sometimes ending suffering takes priority over extending life.* Assisted death is so troubling because it involves an agonizing conflict between values. Life is a wonderful gift full of the promise of pleasure, joy, happiness, and love. But circumstances may turn it into a heartbreaking, hopeless burden filled with suffering, pain, and despair. We desire to live, but in some situations death may be preferable to the continuation of an intolerably burdensome existence. If some person comes to that dreadful conclusion, what is our duty? The moral imperative forbids us to kill, but it also enjoins us to be merciful. We have a term that puts the dilemma before us—mercy killing. While insisting that we must make every effort possible to guard against abuse, I sorrowfully conclude that, at a patient's request, it may sometimes be more merciful and loving to end suffering than to extend a joyless, unendurable life.

4. *When death becomes preferable to life, everyone would benefit if it were legal to show mercy.* Compassion and benevolence demand that we legalize assisted death for

the sake of the afflicted and those who love them. The most powerful argument in favor of physician-assisted death comes from the families of those who have witnessed loved ones die in extreme agony. When medical science has done all it can and death has not yet brought merciful relief, family members suffer a sense of powerlessness and despair as they watch in horror someone they love dearly writhe in torment as they wait and hope for a quick end to their awful suffering. That these extreme cases are rare is indeed fortunate, but it does not render less important the appalling plight of whose who must live—hopeless and helpless—through such distress. It would benefit everyone if choosing death in hopeless, intolerable situations were allowed under defined circumstances that prevent abuse.

Driven to Extremes

The most forlorn of all are those who agonize over whether to take action in violation of the law to end the life of someone dear to them who pleads and prays for death. A few in desperation, unable to stand it any longer, take a gun or a pillow and do what they dread and hate to do but must do in order to bring relief to a parent or child or spouse who is glad for the intervention but is fearful of the legal consequences for those who have shown them mercy.

You have seen them, or heard them, or read about them. Their faces are sometimes hidden and their voices are disguised as they tell their sad stories. They must witness in secret to what has happened because the law condemns their compassion and calls them murderers. Yet they loved the deceased with all their hearts and were moved to do the dreadful deed out of pure benevolence.

Physicians are more fortunate in that they can take refuge in the principle of the "double effect" and write on the death certificate the cause of death. Many of us have heard doctors report that they have, out of compassion and mercy, given heavy doses of morphine to relieve the intolerable distress of patients who are near to an inevitable death, knowing full well that the result will be to hasten the end. Somehow this is all right, since the primary aim is, we say, to relieve suffering and not to kill, but it would not be right, we are told, to do the very same thing with the primary aim of hastening death, while getting the secondary result of comfort.

Why do we force good people full of love, mercy, and compassion to such extreme measures to bring an end to hopeless torment when no cure or relief is possible for the dearest people on earth to them? Why do we force physicians to justify their mercy in hastening death by denying that they did it for that reason, when we all know what is really going on?

I am a theologian, a philosopher, an ethicist, and a Baptist minister. I hold our moral, legal, and theological heritage in high regard. But there are times when we need to rethink received wisdom by subjecting our principles, codes, and traditions to a fresh exposure to real life experience. Sometimes ideals that are designed to protect and enhance life may actually degrade life and be the source of unnecessary suffering. So it is I believe with the prohibition of physician-assisted death under any and all circumstances. We can provide an opportunity for patients in certain extreme and rare cases under strictly regulated conditions to manage their dying without endangering our reverence for life. In so doing we can provide a way to be merciful to the dying without branding those who show mercy as criminals. We can avoid the agony of family members and of physicians who must do in secret what love and compassion urge upon them and thus serve the dying while honoring the living.

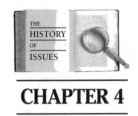

THE
HISTORY
OF
ISSUES

CHAPTER 4

Physicians and Assisted Suicide

Chapter Preface

The power of doctors to extend life and stave off death creates a dilemma. If they consent to a suffering patient's request for assisted suicide, they participate in killing, which is anathema to their profession. Doctors who oppose physician-assisted suicide argue that all physicians take the Hippocratic Oath to never aid in a patient's death. At the same time, some doctors argue that an incurably ill patient who is in great pain, wants to hasten death, and requests lethal pills should have access to assistance to end needless suffering and die with dignity.

Supporters of physician-assisted suicide agree with its aim of promoting personal autonomy or self-determination at the end of life. To them, "choice" is a key word. Faye J. Girsh of the Hemlock Society asserts that how an individual chooses to die is "the final decision [he or she] makes," and "there must be autonomy at that time of life." Timothy E. Quill, a New York–based internist who recommends assisted suicide only as a last resort, advocates "working with individuals at the end of their life and . . . trying to give them as much choice as possible."

Doctors who oppose assisting in suicide maintain that the practice is a form of killing, and therefore violates the values of medicine, which is concerned with preserving life. This is the position of the American Medical Association (AMA). Similarly, bioethicist Daniel Callahan argues that doctors should "relieve pain, do what they can to allay anxiety and uncertainty," but that it is not their "place to lift from us the burden of that suffering which turns on the meaning we assign to the decay of the body and its eventual death. It is not medicine's place to determine when lives are not worth living or when the burden of life is too great to be borne." A senior associate for health policy at the Hastings Center, a research and education organization which he helped found, Callahan calls physician-assisted suicide "self-determination run amok."

In the following chapter, the two sides of the debate are elucidated by physicians with active medical practices.

Assisting in Suicide Is Part of a Physician's Duty

JACK KEVORKIAN

*The following article is Jack Kevorkian's acceptance speech
for the 1994 Humanist Hero Award from the American Humanist Association. Kevorkian, a pathologist from Michigan
who became known in the 1990s for his extraordinary methods in carrying out assisted suicide, argues that it is his role
as a physician to help those who are in pain and want to end
their lives. Kevorkian, who has been variously dubbed by the
media as "Dr. Death," "angel of mercy," and "suicide crusader," defends his practice by arguing that ethical principles
are not universal or eternal. In other words, it is not always
ethical to try to preserve life at all costs when someone is suffering. Sometimes the right thing to do is to help a person end
a painful life. Kevorkian, who almost single-handedly made
physician-assisted suicide a national issue in the 1990s, attributes the opposition to assisted suicide to what he calls a
conspiracy among the medical community, the pharmaceutical industry, and organized religion. Kevorkian's career of
assisting suicide spanned a decade, during which he helped
some 130 people end their lives, using a machine he had designed. After Michigan revoked his medical license in 1991,
blocking his access to lethal drugs, he used carbon monoxide
to help people end their lives. At the time of writing, Kevorkian was facing indictment for two counts of murder. In his*

speech, Kevorkian claims that he is not perturbed by the indictment and vows to continue his work. In 1999, Kevorkian was convicted of murder by a Michigan court and is currently serving a prison sentence.

This is probably the first time that this august body has been addressed by someone under indictment on two counts of first-degree murder.

I was ignorant of many things when I graduated from college. I was uneducated; maybe I still am. All I was trained for was a craft. I think that's true of colleges generally in this country today—they train you for a craft. But everything of value I learned in my life I learned after college, on my own: philosophy, music. . . . The one deficiency I have is literature; I'm very weak there.

So I wasn't attuned, back then, to what life in our society is. I was put by fortune into this position, which has given me a real deep insight into what so-called civilized society is. And I learned one thing: that society is not civilized. And I learned another thing: that we are still deeply mired in the Dark Ages.

Superhighways crossing each other at several levels, color television sets and compact discs, these to me don't indicate the height of civilization, and they don't indicate enlightenment either—in fact, they're dangerous tools of the Dark Ages.

The Inquisition is still alive and well. The only difference is that today it's much more dangerous and subtle. The inquisitors don't burn you at the stake anymore; they slowly sizzle you. They make sure you pay dearly for what you do. In fact, they kill you often in a subtle way. My situation is a perfect example of it.

This is not self-pity, understand. I don't regret the position I'm in. I am not a hero, either—by my definition, anyway. To me, anyone who does what *should* be done is not a hero. Heroes to me are very, very rare. And I still feel that

I'm only doing what I, as a physician, should do. A license has nothing to do with it; I am a physician and therefore I will act like a physician whenever I can. That doesn't mean that I'm more compassionate than anyone else, but there is one thing I am that many aren't and that's honest.

To me, the biggest deficiency today and the biggest problem with society is dishonesty. It underlies almost every crisis and every problem you can name. It's almost an inevitable thing; in fact, it's unavoidable as you mature. Children are honest—born perfectly honest—and slowly learn how to become dishonest. They are trained at it. We feel that a little dishonesty greases the wheels of society, that it makes things easier for everybody if we lie a little to each other. But all this dishonesty becomes cumulative after awhile. If everyone were perfectly honest at all times, if human nature were such that it could stand that, you would find many fewer problems in the world. I know that's impractical. Maybe I'm a hopeless idealist. But at least that's looking at the problem at its root. Children, by the way, can handle honesty. They swear and curse at each other, and it doesn't affect them very much. But it's difficult to be perfectly honest as an adult.

I never considered myself a humanist. I'm not a joiner. I never join any organization. And yet humanism, I think, is the closest to what I think is a good way of living in society.

What is the best rule for life? I often ask myself that. Some people will tell you that "the Golden Rule is the best." Well, I don't know—is it? We spout platitudes without thinking. We're trained not to think, really; we're trained to respond to platitudes. Education does that. I think education in this society is geared toward making sure you are well brainwashed by the time you are an adult.

The Golden Rule: "Do unto others as you would have them do unto you." But that doesn't always apply. What if I met a masochist or a sadist? You see, it wouldn't work. I think the best rule for life is "Say and do what you wish, whenever you wish, so long as you do not harm another person or his or her property." Does that sound right? Now if every adult human being acted that way, this would be a much better society. We may not have color television sets, and we may not have superhighways, but we would probably be a better society. We certainly wouldn't have the Inquisition.

Doing a Physician's Role

So all I'm doing is what a physician should do. I'm not really frightened by what's happening to me; I'm not even intimidated. I'm annoyed! In fact, I'm reinforced in what I'm doing because of the opposition, which is so irrational. . . .

When we first started this work, we didn't expect the explosion of publicity that followed. We tried to keep this low key. I have been accused of grandstanding, recklessness, and publicity seeking, all of which, of course, is not true. You must understand that the entire mainstream media, especially in the first year or two, were totally against what I'm doing. Entirely! It was unanimous. They tried to make my work look very negative—they tried to make *me* look negative—so that they could denigrate the concept we're working on. They said I should not be identified with the concept, yet they strived to do just that. They insulted and denigrated me and then hoped that it would spill over onto the concept. It didn't work, however; according to the polls, people may be split 50-50 on what they think of me, but they are three-to-one in favor of the concept, and that's never changed.

Now isn't it strange that on a controversial subject of this magnitude—one which cuts across many disciplines— the entire editorial policy of the country is on one side? Doesn't that strike you as strange? Even on a contentious issue like abortion, there is editorial support for both sides. And our issue—death with dignity—as far as we're concerned, is simpler than abortion. So why is every mainstream editorial writer and newspaper in the country against us on this? Not one has come out in wholehearted support of us, even though public opinion is on our side.

A Conspiracy over Money

As I surmise it, they're in a conspiracy, which is not a revelation to many people. But with whom? Well, let's take a look at who's against this: organized religion, organized medicine, and organized big money. Now, that's a lot of power.

Why is organized medicine against this? For a couple of reasons, I think: first, because the so-called profession—which is no longer a profession; it's really a commercial enterprise and has been for a long time—is permeated with religious overtones. The basis of so-called medical ethics is religious ethics. The Hippocratic Oath [forbidding physicians in aiding suicide] is a religious manifesto—Pythagorean (pagan, by the way)—they don't even mind that. It is not medical. Hippocrates didn't write it; we don't know who did, but we think it's from the Pythagoreans. So, if you meet a physician who says, "Life is sacred," be careful: we didn't study sanctity in medical school. You are talking to a theologian first, probably a business person second, and a physician third.

The second reason that organized medicine is against physician-assisted voluntary euthanasia is because of the money involved. If a patient's suffering is curtailed by three weeks, can you imagine how much that adds up to in the medical and health-care field? Let's look at Alzheimer's disease. They say, "Well, that's not terminal." Well, it is terminal. Any process that curtails natural life is a terminal disease; the duration of the terminal process is the only difference. Some cancers last a week in their terminal phase. Alzheimer's disease is terminal. I understand that we have four million Alzheimer's cases in this country. Let's assume that one out of ten opts to end his or her life at a certain stage, just when it is getting bad. That's 400,000 people depriving some nursing homes of perhaps four or five years of care for a vegetating human being. At $30,000 a year, multiplied by 400,000, times five years—you're into billions of dollars. And that's just one disease, and one out of ten people.

How about the pharmaceutical industry? A lot of drugs

are used in those last several months and years of life, which also add up to billions and billions of dollars. So you can see why they are going to oppose this.

That's what is so dismaying to me; that's what makes me cynical. You have to be cynical in life when you read about a situation that's so terrible and so incorrigible. There are certain ways to deal with it: you can go along with it, which is hard to do; you can go insane, which is a refuge (and some do that); or you can face it with deep cynicism. I've opted for cynicism.

In responding to the religious issues, I ask this: why not let all the religious underpinnings of medicine apply only to the ethics of religious hospitals and leave the secular hospitals alone? It's a perfect solution. We're not going to tell the religious hospitals what to do; they can perform any insanity they wish. But what they can't do is impose that insanity on the rest of us. The doctors who work in those religious hospitals can refuse to do abortions, they can refuse assisted suicide or euthanasia, they can do anything they want. But they have no right to impose what *they* call a universal medical ethic on secular institutions.

What Is Right at a Certain Time

Besides, what is ethics? Can you define it? My definition is simple: ethics is saying and doing what is right, at the time. Does that make sense? And that changes. Notice I added "at the time.". . .

Ethics is saying and doing what is right at the time and that changes. Geoffrey [Fieger, Kevorkian's lawyer] and I use the example of coal as fuel. Seventy-five years ago, If I told you that for Christmas I was going to have a truck deliver 10 tons of coal to your house, you would have been delighted. If I told you that today, you would be insulted. Doing the right thing changes with time.

That's true of human society also. There is a primitive society—I don't know which one exactly—whose members were shocked to learn that we embalm our dead, place them in boxes, and then bury them in the ground. Do you know what they do? They eat them. To them, it's ethical and moral and honorable to devour the corpse of your loved one. Now we're shocked at that, right? It's all a matter of acculturation, time, where you are, and who you are. Now if I visited this primitive society and learned that they do that, and I was a real humanist, I'd say, "Oh, that's interesting." And if the so-called savage in turn said, "Gee, that's interesting what you do," then he or she would be a humanist. I used to define maturity as the inability to be shocked. So I guess in some ways we're still immature. But if you're truly mature, and a true humanist, you can never be shocked. If they eat their dead, so be it—that's their culture. But you know what our missionaries did, don't you? That's immoral action. . . .

This indictment [of two counts of first-degree murder] has done one good thing, however: it brazenly manifests the depth of corruption within our society. And it's not just the judiciary. Our legislature has manifested that as well with its silly law which it knew was unconstitutional. What kind of a legislature or government is it that would enact a so-called law it knew was unconstitutional? Can anybody get more depraved than that? Or more corrupt? Hardly. But that corruption permeates everything.

Our medical societies are just as corrupt; our medical boards are just as corrupt. I don't have a license any more. Did that stop me from doing what a physician should do? No! You see, the licensure is not entirely to guarantee competence. In fact, I think that's only a small part of what licensure is supposed to do. It guarantees absolute control. But they miscalculated on me. A piece of paper does not control me. They can't take away my training, my experience, or what I want to do, what I feel is right. They miscalculated, and now their anger knows no bounds. That is why they are behaving the way they are. That is why you are seeing so much negative press. They are desperate now, and that makes them dangerous. When anyone becomes that desperate, they are dangerous, and I recognize the danger.

So you see, in effect, our society is no different than primitive society—or Nazi Germany. People easily forget that. We pride ourselves in this country and the Western world, saying, "We're really enlightened and we're different." No, we're still totalitarian to a great degree. . . .

I hate to end on a pessimistic note, but I appreciate this opportunity to address you all. I thank you for your support. We are very much encouraged by it. We will keep going.

Physician-Assisted Suicide Subverts the Role of Doctors as Healers

LONNIE R. BRISTOW

Lonnie R. Bristow is the president of the American Medical Association (AMA). In the following selection, Bristow explains the organization's opposition to physician-assisted suicide, stating that the practice is unethical and incompatible with the physician's role as healer. The AMA believes that physician-assisted suicide could cause a great deal of harm because its practice would be difficult to control. One problem is possible discrimination against incompetent patients (such as those in comas who cannot communicate) who have not indicated their wishes in clear terms, as well as other vulnerable populations, including the elderly and people with disabilities. The AMA makes a distinction between the withdrawal of medical treatment and the active use of medical procedures and skills to cause death. The AMA does not oppose the withdrawal of extraordinary medical treatment when a competent patient requests it, but it objects to proposals that would have physicians actively hastening death. Instead of assisted suicide, the AMA recommends that doctors provide adequate pain control and emotional support for the terminally ill. Bristow presented the AMA's position to the Committee on the Judiciary of the U.S. House of Repre-

Lonnie R. Bristow, statement before the Subcommittee on the Constitution, House Committee on the Judiciary, April 29, 1996.

sentatives on April 29, 1996. Based in California at the time, he practiced internal medicine and lectured on medical science and the socioeconomic and ethical aspects of medicine. The AMA, founded in 1847, is a professional organization that advocates for physicians and patients. The organization has provided testimony and expert advice to courts on numerous cases involving euthanasia.

For nearly 2,500 years, physicians have vowed to "give no deadly drug if asked for it, [nor] make a suggestion to this effect." What has changed, that there should be this attempt to make "assisted suicide" an accepted practice of medicine? Certainly the experience of physical pain has not changed over time. Yet the blessings of medical research and technology present their own new challenges, as our ability to delay or draw out the dying process alters our perceptions and needs.

Our efforts in this new paradigm must recognize the importance of care that relieves pain, supports family and relationships, enhances functioning, and respects spiritual needs. Calls for legalization of physician-assisted suicide point to a public perception that these needs are not being met by the current health care system. In addition, society has not met its responsibility to plan adequately for end-of-life care. It is this issue—how to provide quality care at the end of life—which the AMA [American Medical Association] believes should be our legitimate focus.

The AMA believes that physician-assisted suicide is unethical and fundamentally inconsistent with the pledge physicians make to devote themselves to healing and to life. Laws that sanction physician-assisted suicide undermine the foundation of the patient-physician relationship that is grounded in the patient's trust that the physician is working wholeheartedly for the patient's health and welfare. The multidisciplinary members of the New York State Task Force on Life and the Law concur in this belief, writing that "physician-assisted suicide and euthanasia violate values that are fundamental to the practice of medicine and the patient-physician relationship."

Yet physicians also have an ethical responsibility to relieve pain and to respect their patient's wishes regarding care, and it is when these duties converge at the bedside of a seriously or terminally ill patient that physicians are torn.

The AMA believes that these additional ethical duties require physicians to respond aggressively to the needs of the patients at the end of life with adequate pain control, emotional support, comfort care, respect for patient autonomy and good communications.

Further efforts are necessary to better educate physicians in the areas of pain management and effective end-of-life care. Patient education is the other essential component of an effective outreach to minimize the circumstances which might lead to a patient's request for physician-assisted suicide: inadequate social support; the perceived burden to family and friends; clinical depression; hopelessness; loss of self-esteem; and the fear of living with chronic, unrelieved pain.

Ethical Considerations

The physician's primary obligation is to advocate for the individual patient. At the end of life, this means the physician must strive to understand the various existential, psychological, and physiological factors that play out over the course of terminal illness and must help the patient cope with each of them. Patients who are understandably apprehensive or afraid of their own mortality need support and comforting, not a prescription to help them avoid the issues of death. Patients who believe sudden and "controlled" death would protect them from the perceived indignities of prolonged deterioration and terminal illness must receive social support as well as the support of the profession to work through these issues. Providing assisted suicide would breach the ethical means of medicine to safeguard patients' dignity and independence.

Many proponents of assisted suicide cite a fear of prolonged suffering and unmanageable pain as support for their position. For most patients, advancements in palliative care can adequately control pain through oral medications, nerve blocks or radiotherapy. We all recognize, however, that there are patients whose intractable pain cannot be relieved by treating the area, organ or system perceived as the source of the pain. For patients for whom pain cannot be controlled by other means, it is ethically permissible for physicians to administer sufficient levels of controlled substances to ease pain, even if the patient's risk of addiction or death is increased.

The failure of most states to expressly permit this practice has generated reluctance among physicians to prescribe adequate pain medication. Additional uncertainty is produced by the potential for legal action against the physician when controlled substances are prescribed in large amounts to treat patients with intractable pain. This uncertainty chills physicians' ability to effectively control their terminally ill patients' pain and suffering through the appropriate prescription and administration of opiates and other controlled substances. In this area, states such as California and Texas have developed clear legislative guidance that resolves these concerns for most physicians. The AMA is developing similarly structured model legislation for state medical societies to pursue with their state legislatures and medical licensing boards.

In some instances, administration of adequate pain medication will have the secondary effect of suppressing the respiration of the patient, thereby hastening death. This is commonly referred to as the "double effect." The distinction between this action and assisted suicide is crucial. The physician has an obligation to provide for the comfort of the patient. If there are no alternatives but to increase the risk of death in order to provide that comfort, the physician is ethically permitted to exercise that option. In this circumstance, the physician's clinical decision is guided by the intent to provide pain relief, rather than an intent to cause death. This distinguishes the ethical use of palliative care medications from the unethical application of medical skills to cause death.

Distinction Between Withholding or Withdrawing Treatment and Assisted Suicide

Some participants in the debate about assisted suicide see no meaningful distinction between withholding or withdrawing treatment and providing assistance in suicide. They argue that the results of each action are the same and therefore the acts themselves carry equal moral status. This argument largely ignores the distinction between act and omission in the circumstances of terminal care and does not address many of the principles that underlie the right of patients to refuse the continuation of medical care and the duty of physicians to exercise their best clinical judgment.

Specifically, proponents who voice this line of reasoning fail to recognize the crucial difference between a patient's right to refuse unwanted medical treatment and any proposed right to receive medical intervention which would cause death. Withholding or withdrawing treatment allows death to proceed naturally, with the underlying disease being the cause of death. Assisted suicide, on the other hand, requires action to cause death, independent from the disease process.

The "Slippery Slope"

Physician-assisted suicide raises troubling and insurmountable "slippery slope" problems. Despite attempts by some, it is difficult to imagine adequate safeguards which could effectively guarantee that patients' decisions to request assisted suicide were unambivalent, informed and free of coercion.

A policy allowing assisted suicide could also result in the victimization of poor and disenfranchised populations who may have greater financial burdens and social burdens which could be "relieved" by hastening death. As reported two years ago [1994] by the New York State Task Force on Life and the Law (composed of bioethicists, lawyers, clergy and state health officials), "[a]ssisted suicide and euthanasia will be practiced through the prism of social inequality and prejudice that characterizes the delivery of services in all segments of society, including health care."

Recent studies documenting reasons for patient requests for physician-assisted suicide speak to our "slippery slope" concerns. Patients were rarely suffering intractable pain. Rather, they cited fears of losing control, being a burden, being dependent on others for personal care and loss of dignity often associated with end-stage disease.

The Case of the Netherlands

While euthanasia and assisted suicide are not legal in the Netherlands [as of 1996; in 2001, they were legalized] comprehensive guidelines have been established which allow physicians to avoid prosecution for the practice. Despite this environment, Dutch physicians have become uneasy about their active role in euthanasia, prompting the Royal Dutch Medical Association to revise its recommendations on the practice.

Findings of more than 1,000 cases of involuntary euthanasia in the Netherlands should raise hackles in the United States, particularly given the stark societal differences between the two countries. Health coverage is universal in the Netherlands, the prevalence of long-term patient-physician relationships is greater and social supports are more comprehensive. The inequities in the American healthcare system, where the majority of patients who request physician-assisted suicide cite financial burden as a motive, make the practice of physician-assisted suicide all the more unjustifiable. No other country in the world, including the Netherlands, has legalized assisted suicide or euthanasia. This is one movement in which the United States should not be a "leader."

Educating Physicians and Patients

At its last meeting in December of 1995, the AMA House of Delegates adopted recommendations from a report issued by its Task Force on Quality Care at the End of Life. The report identified issues involved with care of the dying, including the need to develop a definition of "futility," provision of optimal palliative care, legislation ensuring access to hospice benefits, and the importance of advance care planning as a part of standard medical care. Based on the report's recommendations, the AMA is coordinating its current efforts and developing a comprehensive physician and patient education outreach campaign regarding quality of care at the end of life.

The AMA is uniquely capable of educating physicians and other caregivers, legislators, jurists, and the general public as to end-of-life care issues. Recognizing the profession's desire to structure discussions of end-of-life care and maintain an active and improved role in the care of dying patients, the AMA is currently designing a comprehensive physician education outreach to instruct physicians in conducting advance care planning and managing palliative care with their patients. In fostering such communication, the AMA is particularly concerned with enabling physicians to support patient autonomy, providing patients with sufficient background and support to make informed decisions regarding their end-of-life treatment.

In October of 1995, the AMA, with the American Bar Association (ABA) and the American Association of Retired Persons (AARP), jointly published the booklet "Shaping Your Health Care Future," which offers information about advance care planning and a portable model advance directive for physicians and their patients. The guide also provides explicit instructions for including expressed wishes in the patient's record to ensure that they will be honored. A copy accompanies this testimony. The AMA is working with HCFA [Health Care Financing Administration] to facilitate distribution of this valuable resource to Medicare enrollees. We are also in discussion with the U.S. Consumer Information Center to promote broader public distribution of the booklet.

In supporting professional education, the AMA's continuing medical education division, in cooperation with the United States Air Force Reserve, produced a four-part video series, "The Ethical Question: Decisions Near the End of Life." The videos include discussions of patient autonomy, awareness of legal requirements, allocation of scarce resources and emphasis on compassionate care. Such videos are valuable educational tools, stimulating thoughtful discussion physician to patient or with groups of either patients or physicians. The AMA was also actively involved in the development of the Education Development Corporation workshop, "Decisions Near the End of Life," an institution-based program to train caregivers facing ethical decisions regarding dying patients.

Through continued educational efforts, physicians are committed to demonstrating their enduring commitment to providing the best patient care during every stage of life. Furthermore, provided the tools to facilitate improved terminal care, physicians can readily answer many of the arguments of assisted suicide's proponents. . . .

The movement for legally sanctioning physician-assisted suicide is a sign of society's failure to address the complex issues raised at the end of life. It is not a victory for personal rights. We are equipped with the tools to effectively manage end-of-life pain and to offer terminally ill patients dignity and to add value to their remaining time. As the voice of the medical profession, the AMA offers its capability to coordinate multidisciplinary discourse on end-of-life issues, for it is essential to coordinate medical educators, patients, advocacy organizations, allied health professionals and the counseling and pastoral professions to reach a comprehensive solution to these challenging issues. Our response should be a better informed medical profession and public, working together to preserve fundamental human values at the end of life.

Patients Need Better End-of-Life Care Rather than Assisted Suicide

KATHLEEN FOLEY

In this article, Kathleen Foley declares there is an alternative to assisted suicide that is not being adequately addressed by the health care system in the United States: quality care for patients with life-threatening illness. She argues that policy makers should adopt reforms in the health care system to ensure that high-quality, acceptable palliative care is made available in hospitals and nursing homes, where the majority of American adults die. Unendurable pain is often the reason patients request assisted suicide, but Foley argues that palliative care is a more compassionate way of alleviating their pain than helping them to commit suicide. Foley is a professor of neurology, neuroscience, and clinical pharmacology at Weill Medical College of Cornell University and an attending neurologist at the Pain and Palliative Care Service of the Memorial Sloan-Kettering Cancer Center in New York. In 1996, she was the director of the World Health Organization Collaborating Center for Cancer Pain Research and Education. She is the coeditor (with Herbert Hendin) of The Case Against Assisted Suicide: For the Right to End-of-Life Care.

Kathleen Foley, *The Case Against Assisted Suicide: For the Right to End-of-Life Care*, edited by Kathleen Foley and Herbert Hendin. Baltimore, MD: The Johns Hopkins University Press, 2002. Copyright © 2002 by The Johns Hopkins University Press. All rights reserved. Reproduced by permission.

The physician-assisted suicide debate in the United States has called attention to a crisis in our health care system: the profound inadequacy of the care of chronically ill and dying patients. In a 1997 report entitled *Approaching Death*, the Institute of Medicine of the National Academy of Sciences reviewed the medical, social, economic, and institutional factors preventing Americans from receiving appropriate, humane, compassionate care at the end of life. . . .

The World Health Organization (WHO) [has] identified the inadequate care of patients with incurable cancer as well as other diseases as a serious national and international public health problem requiring the development of programs in palliative care. An international panel defined palliative care as "the active total care of patients whose disease is not responsive to curative therapies." Control of pain, psychosocial distress, and existential, religious, and cultural issues is the focus of care emphasizing the patient's quality of life not quantity of life. This approach is patient- and family-centered and should be part of any primary care health system. The term *palliative* was chosen to be inclusive of hospice and supportive care programs, and to describe a broad health care delivery system that could be either hospital- or home-based and widely applicable to all patients with incurable diseases.

Moreover, the WHO expert panel dearly distinguished palliative care from physician-assisted suicide and euthanasia and included as one of its major recommendations that "member states not consider legislation allowing for physician assisted suicide or euthanasia until they had assured for their citizens the availability of services for pain relief and palliative care."

In 1999 the Council of Europe issued recommendations on the care of the dying, fully supporting the WHO recommendations and arguing strongly that palliative care programs are needed. The Council cited the European Convention on Human Rights, Article 2, which states that "no one shall be deprived of his life intentionally." Of note, all of these documents conceptualize the care of those who are dying as a societal issue, not merely a medical issue, and all have called for broad participation of all members of society in addressing the care of the dying as a public health issue. Thus discussion on the legalization of physician-assisted suicide needs to address the quality, availability, and acceptability of the current options of care for patients with serious life-threatening illness. . . .

A Complex Problem

What has emerged in this debate in the last ten years is that physician-assisted suicide, and care at the end of life, are complex social and medical problems. Physician-assisted suicide was initially pictured as a compassionate response to the need for "balancing a reverence for life with the belief that death should come with dignity." In the last five years, perceptions have shifted, and many now view physician-assisted suicide as a potentially cost-effective way to limit care to a marginalized, chronically ill population of patients.

The portrayal of this debate in the public press was initially galvanized by [retired Michigan pathologist Jack] Kevorkian, who portrayed end-of-life symptoms, such as pain, as untreatable and unbearable, and physician-assisted suicide as the only option for patients who were suffering needlessly. This clearly encouraged a public perception that death is always painful and that individuals need to control their own dying because medical institutions and health care professionals will either keep them alive too long or let them die without control of pain or other symptoms. When Kevorkian administered a lethal drug dose to a disabled patient with amyotrophic lateral sclerosis (ALS) and shared the videotape of this experience with the American public on *60 Minutes*, the media focused on the fact that the simple way to address suffering in those who are disabled or who have incurable disease is to kill the sufferer. Little media attention was given to the options for care of patients with ALS to improve the quality of their living as they are dying.

Similarly, decisions by the Second and Ninth Circuit Courts of Appeals that reversed state bans (in New York and Washington) on assisted suicide used language that showed little respect for the vulnerability and dependence of dying patients. Judge Stephen Reinhardt, ruling for the Ninth Circuit, applied "the liberty interest clause" of the Fourteenth Amendment and advocated a constitutional right to assisted suicide. He stated that "the competent terminally ill adult having lived nearly the full measure of his life has a strong interest in choosing a dignified and humane death rather than being reduced to a state of helplessness, diapered, sedated, and incompetent." This statement enraged disabled persons, who argued that even in their helpless, diapered, and incompetent state, they were both dignified and humane. Judge Roger J. Miner, writing for the Second Circuit Court of Appeals, applied the equal rights clause of the Fourteenth Amendment and went on to emphasize that the state has no interest in prolonging a life that is ending. This statement is more than legal jargon; it serves as a chilling reminder of the low priority given to the dying when it comes to state resources and protection.

Public advocacy and legal cases involving physician-assisted suicide have provided a unique opportunity to engage the public, health care professionals, and the government in a national discussion on how American medicine and society should address the needs of dying patients and their families. Such a discussion is critical if we are to understand the process of dying from the point of view of patients and their families and identify existing barriers to appropriate, humane, compassionate care at the end of life. Rational discourse needs to replace the polarized debate over physician-assisted suicide and euthanasia, and facts, not anecdotes, are necessary to establish a common ground and frame a system of health care for the terminally ill that provides the best possible quality of living for those who are dying.

Epidemiology and Ethnography of Dying

What are the facts? In the United States, approximately 2.5 million people die each year. We have almost no information on how they die and only general information on where they die: 71 percent die in hospitals, 17 percent die in nursing homes, and the remainder (10 percent to 14 percent of whom are receiving hospice care) die at home. . . .

With the majority of adults in the United States now dying in hospitals, it has become all too evident that both hospitals and physicians are not equipped or trained to handle the medical and psychosocial problems that face those who are dying and their caregivers. Several studies have categorized the barriers to adequate palliative care programs, ranging from the lack of professional knowledge and skills in palliative care to significant financial and structural barriers in the health care delivery system. Increasing attention has focused on the need to identify the opportunities to improve the delivery of palliative care at the end of life as a first step toward developing corrective approaches and preventing needless suffering. It has been strongly argued that palliative care must become an integral component of primary medical care.

The Goals of Palliative Care

The goals of palliative care include the alleviation of suffering, the optimization of quality of life until death ensues, and the provision of comfort in death. Persistent suffering that is inadequately relieved undermines the value of life for the sufferer. Without hope that this situation will be relieved, patients, their families, and professional caregivers may see euthanasia and assisted suicide as their only alternatives. . . .

Using the cancer patient as an example, an encounter with advanced cancer is a cause of great distress to patients, their families, and professional caregivers attending them. Two-thirds of patients with advanced disease have significant pain; numerous other physical symptoms diminish such patients' quality of life; and many patients endure enormous psychological distress. From an existential perspective, even without pain or other physical symptoms, continued life is without meaning for some patients. For the families and loved ones of patients, there is similar great distress in this process—from anticipating loss, standing witness to the patient's physical and emotional distress, and bearing the burdens of care. Professional caregivers as well may be stressed by the suffering that they witness and that challenges their clinical and emotional resources. On this model, the suffering of each of these groups is highly interrelated, since the perceived distress of any one of these three groups may amplify the distress of the others.

The goal of palliative care is to address the complex issues of suffering from the perspective of the patient and the family and define a system of care appropriate to the needs of the individual patient. This formulation of the therapeutic response requires an understanding of the phenomenon of suffering and the factors that contribute to it. Failure to appreciate or effectively address the full diversity of contributing factors may confound effective therapeutic strategies. The available data suggest that health care professionals—specifically physicians and nurses—are not adequately trained to assess and manage the multifactorial symptoms commonly associated with patients at the end of life and lack training in all aspects of palliative care.

Factors Associated with Suffering in Patients

Three major factors contribute to patients' suffering: pain or other physical symptoms, psychological distress, and existential distress.

Pain Symptoms

Pain is the most common symptom in dying patients; according to recent data from U.S.-based studies, 56 percent of outpatients with cancer, 82 percent of outpatients with

AIDS, 50 percent of hospitalized patients with various diagnoses, 36 percent of nursing home residents with cancer, and 89 percent of children dying of cancer have inadequate management of suffering during the course of their terminal illness. Members of minority groups and women, both those with cancer and those with AIDS, as well as the elderly, receive less pain treatment than other groups of patients. In a survey of 1,177 physicians who treated a total of more than 70,000 patients with cancer in the previous six months 76 percent of the physician respondents reported that lack of knowledge was a barrier to their ability to control pain. Fifty-six percent of these physicians' patients reported moderate to severe pain. Severe pain that is not adequately controlled interferes with patients' quality of life, including activities of daily living, sleep, and social interactions.

Other physical symptoms are prevalent among those who are dying. Studies of patients with advanced cancer, patients with AIDS, and the elderly in the year before death show that they have numerous symptoms that diminish the quality of life, such as fatigue, difficulty breathing, delirium, nausea, and vomiting. Studies in children with cancer demonstrated a comparable number of symptoms.

Psychological Symptoms

Concurrent with these physical symptoms, patients have a variety of well-described psychological symptoms, with a high prevalence of anxiety and depression in elderly patients and those with cancer or AIDS. For example, studies in elderly patients demonstrate that depressive symptoms interfere with their ability to make decisions about resuscitation. More than 60 percent of patients with advanced cancer have psychiatric problems, with adjustment disorders, depression, anxiety, and delirium reported most frequently. . . .

Existential Distress

A third category of suffering that compounds the multiple physical and psychological symptoms terminally ill patients experience is their degree of existential distress. Increasing attention has focused on the need to understand the spiritual, religious, and cultural dimensions of patients' dying experience. A recent survey on spiritual beliefs in the dying process that elicited patients' concerns about not having the opportunity to say goodbye, or being in a vegetative state for a long period of time, or being a burden to their family provides some information about their perspectives on these issues. In a recent focus group study about what was important in care at the end of life, patients cited a variety of concerns, including freedom from pain and the opportunity to choose their place of death. They also pointed out two other factors that had not previously been well identified: their desire to be cared for as "whole persons," with attention to their spiritual, religious, and cultural beliefs, and their wish to be identified as contributing to and maintaining a role in society. No longer having a social role is often described by patients as a major reason they view themselves as a burden not only to their families but to themselves. . . .

Health Care Professionals' Lack of Education

Inadequate response to the complex suffering of dying patients—physical, psychological, and existential—in part results from health care providers' lack of knowledge and education. According to the American Medical Association's report on medical education, only 5 of 126 medical schools in the United States require a separate course in the care of the dying. Of 7,048 residency programs, only 26 percent offer a course on the medical and legal aspects of care at the end of life. In a survey of 1,068 accredited residency programs in family medicine, internal medicine, and pediatrics, and fellowship programs in geriatrics, each resident or fellow coordinated the care of ten or fewer dying patients annually. Almost 15 percent of these programs offer no formal training in end-of-life care. Despite the availability of hospice programs, only 17 percent of the training programs offer hospice rotation, and only half of these programs require a hospice rotation.

In a survey of 55 residency programs and more than 1,400 residents conducted by the American Board of Internal Medicine, the residents were asked to rate their perception of adequate training in care at the end of life. Only 62 percent reported that they had received adequate training in telling patients that they are dying, only 38 percent in describing what the process would be like, and only 32 percent in talking to patients who request assistance in dying or hastened death. Medical textbooks devote less than 1 percent of their content to addressing the care of dying patients. Nurses and social workers are similarly poorly educated. . . .

Other Barriers to Palliative Care

A wide range of institutional, regulatory, and financial barriers to end-of-life care have also been identified, ranging from the lack of a palliative care team or units in hospitals, to excessive regulatory control of the use of pain medications, to the lack of adequate funding in Medicare and private insurance programs for prescription medications critical to symptom control.

For patients dying in hospitals, there is a major effort to discharge them to alternative systems of care—either to home or to a nursing home. Yet these alternatives lack the expert support required to address the needs of this patient population, thus putting enormous burdens on patients and families in both home care agencies and nursing homes. [The organization] SUPPORT demonstrated that one-third of families exhausted their financial resources in caring for a dying elderly family member at home. Conversely, patients dying in hospitals who do not have advanced directives and family proxies may receive aggressive intensive care that is costly and unwanted.

Fewer than 20 percent of all dying patients receive hospice care in the United States, with cancer patients making up more than 50 percent of those who do; 93 percent of hospice patients are white. The Medicare hospice benefit requires that patients be terminally ill with a prognosis of six months or less and willing to give up access to other medical therapies. This capitated benefit forces patients to shift care from their traditional system and often leads to discontinuity and concern about abandonment by their longtime physician. Yet hospice care provides a high level of expertise in pain management and symptom control and provides a team of health professionals trained in palliative care to address patients' physical and psychosocial needs. Increasingly, hospices are being audited because their patients live "too long," raising the specter of fraud and abuse of the hospice benefit. Yet prognostication is fraught with problems. The unintended consequence of this government oversight has been to force hospices into admitting patients often on "the brink of death," limiting their ability to provide their comprehensive care to patients and families early in the dying process.

These are only a few of the barriers that currently limit patients and families from receiving adequate care. Moreover, there is enormous variation in hospice care across the country. The hospice model is predominantly a nurse-centered one, with physician medical directors who see patients infrequently and rely heavily on nursing expertise. Quality standards for hospice and outcomes practice are not established, making it difficult to assure patients and families that they are receiving quality end-of-life care. . . .

Initiatives Toward Improvement

We have a long way to go to improve end-of-life care for patients and to integrate high-quality palliative care and hospice programs into our system of health care delivery. Our current culture marginalizes those who are dying and creates needless suffering. There is now a unique opportunity to improve the care for this population and to address how we should show true respect for their autonomy. Physicians play a unique role in changing the system of care. Communicating effectively with patients, providing psychosocial support, managing symptoms well, and making timely referrals to hospice will improve care and support for patients and families.

Numerous efforts are under way to meet the challenge of institutionalizing humane, compassionate care for the dying. Over the last five years, major educational initiatives for health care professionals and the public, coupled with a broad advocacy effort to change institutional and economic barriers, have allowed for the public discussion so necessary to improve the quality of living for those who are in the process of dying. These programmatic and educational efforts, mark the beginning of a process that holds the promise of revolutionizing the care of patients at the end of life.

When Palliative Care Fails, Assisted Suicide Should Be an Option

TIMOTHY E. QUILL

In the following selection, Timothy E. Quill, a professor of medicine and psychiatry at the University of Rochester in New York, endorses hospice care as an effective way of caring for the dying. However, he also believes that there are instances in which it fails to relieve the extreme suffering of terminally ill patients. Under these circumstances, Quill—experienced in ministering to dying patients—argues that physician-assisted suicide should be made available as a last resort. Quill admits that sanctioning the procedure involves risks, which should be addressed through legislative action, referendum, and legal challenges. Quill, a key figure in the euthanasia movement, sparked the first discussions on legalizing physician-assisted suicide when he wrote an article describing his assistance with a suicide in the New England Journal of Medicine *in 1991. In 1994 he and other supporters challenged the ban on assisted suicide in New York; their case was rejected by the U.S. Supreme Court in 1997. His publications include* A Midwife Through the Dying Process: Stories of Healing and Hard Choices at the End of Life, Caring for Patients at the End of Life: Facing an Uncertain Future Together, *and* Death and Dignity: Making Choices and Taking Charge.

Timothy E. Quill, "Deciding About Death: Physician-Assisted Suicide and the Courts: A Panel Discussion," *Pharos*, vol. 61, Winter 1998. Copyright © 1998 by *Pharos*. Reproduced by permission.

Because it is hard to address the legal and constitutional issues surrounding physician-assisted dying without having some feel for the background clinical and ethical issues, I will begin there. I am a primary care doctor. I am also a hospice doctor. I love the work that I do. And when we use medicine's technology to keep people alive and functioning, even into their nineties, we are doing wondrous work.

But we all know that growing old and getting sick aren't for sissies. Sometimes the very interventions we use to keep people alive longer indirectly prolong their dying. Even where there is much suffering, dying people can find moments of meaning and connection, extraordinary moments to be cherished. And when we can help people achieve a peaceful, calm death, the kind of death we would all like to have, we are doing a wondrous task. This goal should be part of medicine, part of our professional responsibility. But it is not easy: sometimes, dying is filled with medical interventions, many with harsh, unintended consequences, so that people can end up in very hard situations. Physicians have a responsibility to respond to these hard situations, just as we have a responsibility to help our patients experience the good situations.

The Importance of Hospice Care

With [hospice advocate] Elisabeth Kübler-Ross as our symbolic guide, I shall talk first about the hospice or palliative care values that should drive this debate. In acute-care medicine, prolonging life is often our foremost objective, and we ask people to endure considerable suffering in the interest of potential recovery and a return to a meaningful life. You would never ask someone to endure an intensive care unit or harsh chemotherapy unless it were for a higher purpose. In hospice care, we acknowledge that we cannot affect the outcome of the disease or prolong life as we would wish, so we make relief of suffering through aggressive symptom management our highest priority. Fundamental to hospice care is getting to know the person as a unique individual and trying to respond to his or her situation using his or her own values. We want to give this individual all possible choice and control, recognizing, of course, that he or she does not have his or her preferred choices. To a person, all hospice patients would choose to get better or return to meaningful life, if that were in their repertoire.

Hospice care's foremost value to the patient may be non-abandonment. We commit to going through the dying process with the patient, wherever this leads. Whether it takes us to places where palliative care instructs us, or to a place where there are no landmarks, where no one knows what to do, we will go there, regardless. In the latter scenario, we will be with the patient and try to problem-solve. Conversing about physician assistance in dying is reserved for cases in which we have gone through this process with the patient, and in which the patient's end-stage suffering is extreme and intolerable—death is all that awaits.

Real Human Experience Versus Ethical Theory

One way I have participated in this policy debate is by telling stories of real people, stories that point up a tension between real human experience and the law, between clinical practice realities and principled ethics. Let me tell you a story, then. A young woman, a graduate student in religion and psychology and a practicing Buddhist, developed abdominal pain while working on her thesis. In three brief days, she went from worrying that she might have an ulcer to hoping she had a lymphoma—because lymphoma is treatable—to knowing she was dying of gastric cancer. She was offered hospice care because chemotherapy does not work for gastric cancer. But she felt abandoned, and went in desperate search of ways to fight this illness. This is when she became my patient.

Together, she and I explored all options, and she elected to try experimental treatment because, at least, that had *not* been shown *not* to work. But she wanted reassurance that she could stop if the going got too hard. That was easy, ethically and legally: people can choose to stop treatment once we are sure they know what they are giving up. She also wanted to know that, if her dying got to be very bad at the end, I would not let her linger and die an agonizing death. For a practicing Buddhist, how you die—your psychological and spiritual state as you depart this life—has important bearing on how you are reborn in the next. This patient wanted me to help her through her dying, wherever it went. To make such a commitment is hard, because our society draws some sharp distinctions between ways physicians can and cannot help people. But I made that commitment to her, as I do to all of my patients who are dying. Thus reassured, she undertook experimental therapy, surgery, and radiation. None, however, worked very well.

After a month in the hospital, experiencing these interventions, this patient turned to hospice, and, under hospice care, went home to prepare to die. She elected to keep her central line in place because, with no stomach, she could not eat. Her pain was well controlled with morphine infusion. She had a wonderful month: she married her long-time boyfriend; her Buddhist community came to the hospital twice weekly for group meditation in which everyone was invited to participate; she gave away her favorite possessions as mementos. After a month, her symptoms intensified, her pain reaching a level where the medicines to control it would also cloud her consciousness. For a Buddhist, clouded consciousness is not a good thing. She also had intractable nausea and vomiting and an open abdominal wound that was foul-smelling and, to her, humiliating. She was ready to die.

A Last Resort

She knew from our conversations that she had some options. She could discontinue her central line, which supplied fluids. She could accept the sedation that comes with higher doses of pain medicine. After a conversation to make sure she understood her choices, the latter was the way she died over the ensuing four or five days. Her death—a good death—occurred in the course of standard hospice care, using hospice values. But it also involved an explicit decision around ending life. The current national policy debate focuses on methods of response to such explicit decisions. To me, the process of physician and patient working together collaboratively over time is much more important than the specific method whereby death is eased.

Physician-assisted death is a narrow question to be raised only when good palliative care fails. Sometimes palliation fails because we are not doing it well enough. Regardless of where we stand individually in the assisted-death debate, we must work together to remedy the inadequacies in the availability and delivery of good palliative care. We don't teach doctors about palliation as we do about CPR or blood gas analysis. And we tend to offer palliative care very late in an illness, when all else has failed—we must learn to offer it earlier and deliver it longer. We still worry about addiction and overdose with pain medication, and doctors worry about being reviewed; these anxieties lead us to undermedicate dying persons. And we have enormous healthcare access problems in this country, to hospice care in particular. We would never want assisted dying to be an alternative to the best care we can deliver. Finally, we must be very aware of how reimbursement incentives might influence our choices.

Hospice Care Has Limits

But there are inherent limitations to hospice care. We are good at relieving suffering on hospice, but not 100 percent of the time. We must learn to acknowledge the exceptions. If we cannot talk about this, our patients think we shall not face up to the extreme suffering if they are so unlucky as to experience it. Sometimes this suffering arises from uncontrollable physical symptoms. Data about what patients on hospice report about pain relief, or relief of shortness of breath, in the last week of life, are sobering. Despite what doctors and nurses report about achieving good symptom relief for hospice patients in the last week of life, the patients themselves often say that they are still experiencing severe pain and shortness of breath. And, given the psychosocial and spiritual dimensions of suffering, it is unrealistic to expect hospice to relieve all suffering. Finally, the dependency and side effects that people endure over a long dying are simply unacceptable to some. Lying in bed in diapers is an experience outside some people's envelope.

We regularly make life-ending decisions in the hospital. We allow people to stop life-sustaining treatment. We handle this process out in the open by putting our best minds together and making a forthright decision. As in the case I described, we often use escalating doses of opioids at the very end when the patient agrees to accept sedation in exchange for better pain control. This is a middle ground, some edges of which are now being explored. Terminal sedation offers the patient the option to be heavily sedated and then "allowed to die." This is not euthanasia—we are not assisting in a death but, rather, relieving suffering; the patient dies from dehydration or other problems. Allowing people to stop eating and drinking when they want to die is also being explored. People are desperate for some choice consistent with their own values, and these may be creative, allowable options. Finally, we have the question of physician-assisted suicide now under debate in the United States; voluntary active euthanasia is not presently an issue here.

A note about terminology: *suicide* is not the right word to use in these conversations; it is correct technically but incorrect from a *meaning* point of view. *Suicide*, or self-killing, has as a connotation destruction of the self. People requesting a doctor's assistance in dying feel that their personhood, their very self, is being destroyed by their illness. They see death not as self-destruction but, rather, as salvation or as a way of asserting their retraining personhood.

Sanctioning Assisted Death Has Its Risks

What are the risks in changing public policy? There is no risk-free way to proceed. First, sanctioning physician-assisted death might be okay for exceptional cases, such as those I have written about. Most people, unless their religious convictions deem it unacceptable under any and all circumstances, can admit exceptional cases. But if we allow this act to occur in the open, we have to wonder about ordinary practice—ordinary doctors and ordinary patients. Can all of them make these difficult, nuanced decisions? There are many slippery slopes to worry about, but to me the most important is that from voluntary to involuntary. Assisted dying might be a choice that people can make for themselves in real time, but it should not be an option where patients have lost decisional ability and depend on others to choose for them. We still must address the suffering of incapacitated patients, but this is not the way. Sanctioning physician-assisted suicide could lead to subtle or explicit coercion—would there evolve a "duty to die"? And the United States has problems of access to health care in general and to hospice care in particular. It would be obscene if physician-assisted suicide became an option for persons without access to care. Finally, some people worry that this practice would give physicians even more power.

The risks of the current prohibitions deserve careful attention. We fail to acknowledge suffering, which many of our patients have known and seen in their own lives. One bad death affects all who witness it, becoming part of their personal story and one of the places they go when they themselves get sick. If we cannot deal with intractable suffering or pretend it never happens, it becomes very frightening to be a patient.

The cases I have written about reflect a deeper problem: people are afraid of dying badly. And, when you look at the phenomenology of dying, even on hospice, suffering is more complex and challenging than we acknowledge.

Current Prohibitions Make Matters Worse

We also know about a secret practice. In Washington State in a recent year, 16 percent of physicians were explicitly asked to assist somehow in a patient's death; a quarter of those doctors provided patients with potentially lethal medication. This phenomenon is not rare, but it occurs without consultation, without open discussion. All the cards are in the physician's hands, and choices depend on the physician's willingness to take risks or the physician's own values and views on the law. I would not want my future hanging on such unpredictable variables. We should look instead to other values. When a person is dying, straight thinking and honest talk should be paramount. The current legal restrictions muddle clear thinking and discourage honesty. We doctors have learned how to hedge our intentions and to act in purposefully ambiguous ways. This is not the way to administer public policy or encourage us to work with our patients in a straightforward way.

Finally, there is aloneness and abandonment at death. Legally, the physician's safest course is to tell a patient seeking medical assistance in dying, "It's illegal. Doctors don't do this. The AMA [American Medical Association] says we don't do this. You're on your own." This leaves the patient and family to find their own solution. With a change in public policy, we could create a system—guided by hospice principles and values and protected by safeguards and a review process—that would bring this decision-making process into the open.

How do we do this? Legislatures are one avenue. The New York State legislature, however, has had difficulty deciding relatively simple end-of-life matters, much less deciding complex questions such as those about physician-assisted suicide for competent, terminally ill patients.

Referendum is another route. Washington, Oregon, and California have had referenda. While public opinion polls show that two-thirds to three-quarters of the people favor allowing doctors and patients more leeway, referenda on this issue seem to break at about 50-50. And there are problems inherent in referenda. For example, the way the original initiative is written is what you are stuck with as a statute. The Oregon initiative included a fourteen-day waiting period for all patients requesting assistance in dying. For patients suffering *in extremis* at death's door, fourteen days seem fourteen lifetimes. For someone further from imminent death, however, the waiting period may be too short. And yet you are stuck—this is how the law was crafted. Referenda are also costly to conduct and often prompt polarizing political advertising. . . .

The current legal prohibition sends all the wrong messages to doctors taking care of patients. No matter what the Supreme Court decides, and especially if the justices say that we should not do this, we shall need to figure out how to respond. First, how do we improve palliative care for all terminally ill persons? And second, how do we respond to those for whom palliative care fails? If the court says we cannot allow physician-assisted suicide, then how should we respond to this difficult second group? Turning our backs may be legally okay but it is morally unacceptable.

Chronology

B.C.

600–300
The Greeks coin the word *euthanatos*, meaning "good death."

500
The Pythagoreans, a religious sect that believes that the soul is mostly divine and eternal, comes into existence.

421
The Greek physician Hippocrates establishes a medical school that forbids doctors from aiding suicide. The Greek philosopher Aristotle condemns suicide.

399
In Greece, the city-state of Athens convicts the philosopher Socrates for "corrupting" the youth with his teachings and orders him to kill himself by drinking the poison hemlock.

A.D.

410
Saint Augustine, bishop of Hippo, asserts that suicide violates God's commandment against killing, reflecting the period's dominant Christian view.

1200s
Saint Thomas Aquinas, expanding on the Christian view, declares that suicide violates God's authority and a person's duty to his family and community.

1500s

English statesman Sir Thomas More writes *Utopia*, in which the government offers to assist terminally ill people to commit suicide; many scholars believe that More, a devout Catholic, may have been writing a satire.

1600s

British philosopher Francis Bacon coins the word *euthanasia* (Greek, meaning "good death") to refer to natural death; the meaning of *euthanasia* as death caused by another to end suffering did not emerge until the twentieth century.

1777

Scottish philosopher David Hume declares that suicide to end suffering from an incurable terminal illness or disability does not violate God's authority or a person's duty to society.

1828

In the United States, New York passes the first state law that criminalizes assisting in suicide.

1906

In Ohio, a bill—the first in the United States—to legalize voluntary euthanasia performed by physicians on the incurably ill, fails.

1931

In Great Britain, C. Killick Millard, a Leicester health officer, drafts a bill attempting to legalize voluntary euthanasia.

1935

The British Voluntary Euthanasia Society, the first in the world, is organized to promote the legalization of euthanasia.

1936
Millard's 1931 euthanasia draft bill is introduced in the British Parliament but fails.

1938
Charles Francis Potter, a Unitarian minister, organizes the Euthanasia Society in New York to promote the legalization of voluntary and involuntary euthanasia.

1939
At the start of World War II, Nazi Germany conducts a "euthanasia" program that eventually kills thousands of Germans and Jews with physical and mental defects.

1950s–1960s
New technology in science and medicine enables physicians to prolong the lives of dying people. It also muddles the idea of "natural" death.

1957
In Rome, Pope Pius XII declares that the terminally ill may refuse "extraordinary" medical technology if death is imminent; he also says that giving drugs to patients to control pain, even if it shortens their life, is also acceptable.

1967
In Florida, a right-to-die bill, introduced in the legislature, fails. In Britain, the world's first hospice facility, St. Christopher's, is established to provide alternative care to the dying through physical, psychological, and spiritual interventions.

1969
The book *On Death and Dying*, written by Swiss-born psychiatrist Elisabeth Kübler-Ross, becomes a best seller and opens up a discussion on death and dying among Americans.

1973

In the Netherlands, a physician found guilty of assisted suicide by injecting his terminally ill mother with a fatal drug is given a very light punishment; the trial marks the start of decriminalization of physician-assisted suicide and euthanasia in the country. In the United States, the American Hospital Association issues the Patient's Bill of Rights, which includes the right to refuse medical treatment.

1974

The New York–based Euthanasia Society is renamed the Society for the Right to Die. In Connecticut, the first American hospice is established in New Haven.

1975

In Britain, journalist Derek Humphry helps his cancer-stricken wife commit suicide with drugs obtained from a doctor.

1975–1976

In New Jersey, Karen Ann Quinlan, a comatose patient, becomes the subject of a legal battle; refused by the hospital and a lower court to remove her respirator, her parents bring the case to the Supreme Court; the Court finally grants permission to turn off the respirator, citing the constitutional right to privacy. California passes the Natural Death Act into law—the first of its kind—making living wills legally binding.

1977

A Massachusetts court rules that an authorized guardian may refuse life-prolonging chemotherapy on behalf of a severely retarded elderly person suffering from leukemia; this extends the range of incompetent people for whom guardians may refuse treatment.

1978

Derek Humphry publishes *Jean's Way*, an account of his

first wife's death, which he had assisted; British authorities do not prosecute him. Doris Portwood publishes *Commonsense Suicide: The Final Right*, which argues that the elderly might be justified in ending their lives.

1979

The Society for the Right to Die (formerly the Euthanasia Society) splits into two organizations; the other organization, Concern for Dying, grew out of the society's Euthanasia Education Council.

1980

Pope John Paul II issues the *Declaration on Euthanasia*, which opposes mercy killing but allows the refusal of medical treatment when death is imminent and treatment is futile; it also permits the greater use of painkillers to ease pain. In the United States, Humphry and his second wife, Ann Wickett, found the Hemlock Society in California to promote the legalization of physician-assisted suicide and voluntary euthanasia for competent, terminally ill adults.

1981

Humphry publishes *Let Me Die Before I Wake*, which includes information on assisted suicide, including drug dosages and methods.

1982

Baby Doe, a boy born deformed and with Down syndrome, dies of starvation after his parents decide against surgery and tube feeding; the case causes public uproar and prompts President Ronald Reagan to instruct government agencies to provide life-sustaining treatment for deformed newborns.

1983

In the United States, Medicare begins covering hospice care; the federal government requires hospitals to post signs announcing that failure to feed handicapped infants violates federal law. Elizabeth Bouvia, disabled by cerebral palsy and arthritis but not terminally ill, goes to court after a hospital refused to starve her to death; a lower court forbids the starvation, but a higher court allows the hospital to remove her feeding tube.

1984

In the Netherlands, a supreme court rules in favor of voluntary euthanasia if doctors observe the guidelines of the Royal Dutch Medical Society. In the United States, twenty-two states and the District of Columbia put into effect advance-care directives.

1985

The U.S. government requires states receiving federal funds for child abuse prevention to give all infants medical treatment, including nutrition, unless they are terminally ill, irreversibly comatose, or when life support is futile. In New Jersey, the guardian of Claire Conroy, an elderly comatose woman, asks for the removal of her feeding tube; the New Jersey Supreme Court forbids the tube's removal since Conroy has not made an advance directive.

1986

The American Medical Association states that removing both respirator and feeding tubes from a comatose patient is ethical if the person has left an advance directive. The Hemlock Society drafts a law legalizing physician-assisted suicide and voluntary euthanasia for terminally ill, competent adults; it allows these procedures for competent adults who are irreversibly but not terminally ill; it also requires people with early Alzheimer's disease to nominate a surrogate to end their lives when they become incompetent. In California, Americans Against Human Suffering is founded to launch a campaign for assisted suicide; it is instrumental in pushing for the 1992 California Death with Dignity Act.

1988

In the case of Nancy Cruzan, a comatose woman, a Missouri probate court allows her parents to remove her feeding tube; however, the Missouri Supreme Court reverses the decision, citing state interest in life and the fact that the Cruzans had no evidence that Nancy would have wanted the feeding tube disconnected.

1989

The U.S. Supreme Court hears the *Cruzan* case, its first right-to-die case.

1990

Jack Kevorkian assists the suicide of Janet Atkins, a woman suffering from the early stages of Alzheimer's, using a gadget he invented; Atkins becomes the first person to be assisted by Kevorkian in committing suicide; the Michigan Board of Medicine later suspends Kevorkian's license. In the case of Cruzan, the U.S. Supreme Court rules against the removal of the feeding tube as the parents had not provided evidence of their daughter's wishes; however, a new hearing establishes Nancy's previous wishes and enables the Court to permit the removal of the tube; Cruzan dies after that. Congress passes the Patient Self-Determination Act, requiring all hospitals and other health care institutions receiving federal funds to explain to all patients their rights.

1991

Final Exit, a how-to book on assisted suicide written by Derek Humphry, becomes a best seller. The *New England Journal of Medicine* publishes an article by Timothy E. Quill, a New York physician, describing how he helped "Diane," a forty-five-year-old woman with terminal leukemia, commit suicide by prescribing her barbiturates; a grand jury refuses to indict Quill. In Washington State, a referendum on euthanasia and physician-assisted suicide fails.

1992

In *Planned Parenthood v. Casey*, the U.S. Supreme Court reaffirms the right to choose abortion, first claimed in *Roe v. Wade* (1973), asserting that the right is protected by the Constitution. In California, a ballot initiative to legalize physician-assisted suicide and euthanasia for competent, terminally ill adults fails.

1993

The National Conference of Commissioners on Uniform State Laws draws up the Uniform Health Care Decisions Act, which legalizes an advance directive that combines a living will, a durable power of attorney, and instructions about organ donation. In Washington State, the organization Compassion in Dying is established.

1994

The New York State Task Force on Life and Law rejects legalizing physician-assisted suicide, claiming it would harm vulnerable groups. In Washington State, Compassion in Dying, and several physicians and patients contest in court the state ban against assisted suicide; a federal district court declares the ban unconstitutional. In New York State, a group of physicians and patients contest in court the state ban against assisted suicide; a federal district court rules that the ban is constitutional. In Oregon, voters approve a ballot initiative on physician-assisted suicide; the state becomes the first in the United States to legalize actively aided death; right-to-life groups appeal to a federal district court to halt the law's implementation. Advance directives are now achieved in all states and the District of Columbia.

1995

The Ninth Circuit Court upholds the constitutionality of Washington State's prohibition against assisted suicide, overturning an earlier court ruling. In Oregon, a federal district court strikes down the Death with Dignity Act; Oregon appeals the decision. In Australia, the legislature of the

Northern Territory passes the Rights of the Terminally Ill Act, which allows terminally ill people to seek physician-assisted suicide under certain conditions; the federal Parliament votes against it.

1996

The Federal Ninth Circuit Court of Appeals overturns the 1995 ruling that the Washington State ban on assisted suicide is constitutional, citing there is constitutional protection for a "right to die." The Second Circuit Court of Appeals strikes down New York's laws against assisted suicide; the court claims that the laws discriminate against terminally ill people who are not on life support and thus violate the Fourteenth Amendment. The U.S. Supreme Court decides it will review Compassion in Dying cases in both Washington and New York. Not Dead Yet, a militant group of disabled individuals, is organized to resist legalization of assisted suicide.

1997

The U.S. Ninth Circuit Court of Appeals reverses a lower court's ruling against Oregon's Death with Dignity Act. Congress passes the Assisted Suicide Funding Restriction Act, prohibiting federally funded health programs from participating in assisted suicide. In Colombia (South America), a supreme court ruling legalizes euthanasia, making the country the only one in the Americas to do so. The U.S. Supreme Court decides in favor of Washington and New York state laws prohibiting physician-assisted suicide, claiming there is no constitutionally protected "right to die," the Court also instructs the states to continue debates on the matter. In Oregon, a second vote for the Death with Dignity Act paves the way to its enforcement; however, the U.S. Drug Enforcement Administration (DEA) blocks it, warning that physicians prescribing drugs to assist in suicide will be prosecuted under the Controlled Substances Act; in 1998 U.S. attorney general Janet Reno overrules the DEA.

1998

Michigan passes a law criminalizing assisted suicide. Kevorkian is charged with murder in assisting Thomas Youk, a fifty-two-year-old man suffering from amyotrophic lateral sclerosis; Kevorkian is later convicted of murder and is sentenced to ten to twenty-five years in prison. In Switzerland, lawyer Ludwig Minelli founds Dignitas, a non-profit organization that provides assistance to suicide; under Swiss law, assisted suicide is not a criminal act if it is done with an altruistic motive; it remains a controversial issue, but the Swiss public generally supports it.

1999

The American Medical Association launches a program to educate physicians about end-of-life care. The House of Representatives passes the Pain Relief Promotion Act, a revised version of the Lethal Drug Abuse Prevention Act, which contains provisions on hospice and pain-management programs.

2000

In Maine, a citizens ballot initiative approving physician-assisted suicide is defeated.

2001

U.S. attorney general John Ashcroft issues a directive warning that doctors who prescribe painkillers to end a patient's life will be prosecuted under the Controlled Substances Act; Oregon contests the directive in court. The Netherlands legalizes assisted suicide and euthanasia; the law provides that doctors may assist in suicide when a patient suffering from intractable pain has made a request to die and an independent physician has concluded there is no other option.

2002

A federal court rules that the U.S. attorney general does not have the authority to overturn Oregon's law on physician-assisted suicide. In the Netherlands, the law on euthanasia and physician-assisted suicide takes effect; in Belgium, a similar law is passed.

2003

Attorney General John Ashcroft appeals to the Ninth Circuit Court of Appeals to reverse a lower court's decision that Oregon's Death with Dignity Act does not violate federal law.

Organizations to Contact

The editors have compiled the following list of organizations concerned with the topics contained in this book. The descriptions are derived from materials provided by the organizations. All have publications or information available for interested readers. The list was compiled on the date of publication of the present volume; the information provided here may change. Be aware that many organizations take several weeks or longer to respond to inquiries, so allow as much time as possible.

American Academy of Hospice and Palliative Medicine
4700 W. Lake Ave. Glenview, IL 60025-1485
(847) 375-4712 • fax: (877) 734-8671
e-mail: info@aahpm.org • Web site: www.aahpm.org

The academy is an international organization of physicians and other professionals dedicated to the advancement of palliative care of terminally ill patients by providing educational and medical standards, fostering research, and promoting public policy advocacy.

American Civil Liberties Union (ACLU)
132 W. Forty-third St., New York, NY 10036
(212) 994-9800
e-mail: aclu@aclu.org • Web site: www.aclu.org

The ACLU champions the rights of individuals in right-to-die and euthanasia cases, as well as in many other civil rights issues. The ACLU Foundation provides legal defense, research, and education and publishes the quarterly *Civil Liberties* and various pamphlets, books, and position papers.

American Foundation for Suicide Prevention (AFSP)
120 Wall St., 22nd Fl., New York, NY 10005
(888) 333-AFSP • (212) 363-3500 • fax: (212) 363-6237
e-mail: inquiry@afsp.org • Web site: www.afsp.org

AFSP opposes the legalization of physician-assisted suicide. It supports scientific research on depression and suicide, educates the public and professionals on the recognition and treatment of suicidal individuals, and provides support to those coping with the loss of a loved one to suicide. The foundation publishes a policy statement on physician-assisted suicide and a quarterly newsletter.

American Life League
PO Box 1350, Stafford, VA 22555
(540) 659-4171 • fax: (540) 659-2586
e-mail: jjbrown@all.org • Web site: www.all.org

Committed to a pro-life philosophy, the organization seeks to educate Americans on the dangers of all forms of euthanasia and opposes legislative efforts that would legalize or increase its incidence. It publishes a bimonthly pro-life magazine, as well as videos, brochures, and newsletters.

American Medical Association (AMA)
515 N. State St., Chicago, IL 60610
(800) 621-8335
Web site: www.ama-assn.org

The AMA is the nation's largest professional organization for physicians. The association opposes physician-assisted suicide and euthanasia for terminally ill people and supports improvement in palliative care. It publishes the weekly *American Medical News* and the monthly *Journal of the American Medical Association*.

American Nurses Association
600 Maryland Ave. SW, Suite 100 West, Washington, DC 20024
(800) 274-4262 • (202) 651-7000 • fax: (202) 651-7001
e-mail: ethics@ana.org • Web site: www.nursingworld.org

The American Nurses Association opposes physician-assisted suicide and euthanasia. It is the largest professional organization representing registered nurses in the United States.

Americans for Better Care of the Dying
4200 Wisconsin Ave. NW, 4th Fl., Washington, DC 20016
(202) 895-2660 • fax: (202) 966-5410
e-mail: info@abcd-caring.org • Web site: www.abcd-caring.com

Promoting social, professional, and policy reform to improve the care for the terminally ill, the organization works to introduce new methods for delivering end-of-life care and to shape public policy on the same.

American Society of Law, Medicine, and Ethics (ASLME)
765 Commonwealth Ave., Suite 1634, Boston, MA 02215
(617) 262-4990 • fax: (617) 437-7596
e-mail: aslme@bu.edu • Web site: www.aslme.org

ASLME works to provide scholarship, debate, and critical thought to professionals concerned with legal, health care, policy, and ethical issues. It publishes the *Journal of Law, Medicine & Ethics*, as well as a quarterly newsletter.

Association for Death Education and Counselling
342 N. Main St., West Hartford, CT 06117-2507
(860) 586-7503 • fax: (860) 586-7550
e-mail: info@adec.org • Web site: www.adec.org

Seeking to improve the quality of education on death and dying, as well as the quality of end-of-life counseling and caregiving, the association provides information, support, and resources to its members and the public.

The Association for Persons with Severe Handicaps (TASH)
29 W. Susquehanna Ave. Suite 210, Baltimore, MD 21204
(410) 828-8274 • fax: (410) 828-6706
e-mail: nweiss@tash.org • Web site: www.tash.org

This international association of people with disabilities, their families, and advocates seeking to promote the inclusion and participation of all people in society opposes the withholding of food and water from disabled infants and adults on the basis of the judgment of surrogates.

Compassionate Healthcare Network, Canada (CHN International)
11563 Bailey Cres, Surrey, BC V3V 2V4 Canada
(604) 582-3844 • fax: (604) 582-3844
e-mail: chn@intergate.ca • Web site: www.chninternational.com

The network opposes euthanasia, assisted suicide, and other programs and policies that threaten the sick, disabled, infirm, the dying, and the medically at risk. It favors advance directives and improvement in palliative care and provides a variety of educational services.

Compassion in Dying (CID)
6312 SW Capitol Hwy., Suite 415, Portland, OR 97201
(503) 221-9556 • fax: (503) 228-9160
e-mail: info@compassionindying.org
Web site: www.compassionindying.org

CID provides the terminally ill with information on various options at the end of life, including physician-assisted suicide and euthanasia. It provides information on pain management, hospice care, and aid in dying, and advocates laws making aided death available to terminally ill and competent adults.

Death with Dignity National Center
11 Dupont Circle, Suite 202, Washington, DC 20036
(202) 969-1669 • fax: (650) 344-8100
(503) 228-4415 • fax: (503) 228-7454
e-mail: info@dwd.org • Web site: www.dwd.org

The center works to implement a law allowing the terminally ill to hasten their death. It also promotes a comprehensive care system for the terminally ill. In 2003 it joined forces with Oregon Death with Dignity. The center publishes a variety of information, including the pamphlet *Making Choices at the End of Life*.

Disability Rights Education and Defense Fund
2212 Sixth St., Berkeley, CA 94710
(510) 644-2555 • fax: (510) 841-8645
e-mail: dred@dredf.org • Web site: www.dredf.org

In 2003 the organization joined forces with the Oregon Death with Dignity. It works to promote the civil rights and liberties of disabled people through legislation, litigation, advocacy, technical assistance, and education.

Dying with Dignity (Canada)
802-55 Eglinton Ave. East, Suite 705, Toronto, ON M4P 1G8
Canada
(800) 495-6156 • (416) 486-3998 • fax: (416) 486-5562
e-mail: info@dyingwithdignity.ca

Web site: www.dyingwithdignity.ca

The organization works to improve the quality of dying for all Canadians, respecting their own wishes, values, and beliefs. It educates Canadians about their right to choose health care options at the end of life, provides counseling and advocacy services to those who request them, and builds public support for voluntary physician-assisted dying. It publishes a newsletter and maintains an extensive library of euthanasia-related materials that students may borrow.

End-of-Life Choices (formerly the Hemlock Society)
PO Box 101810, Denver, CO 80250-1810
(800) 247-7421 • fax: (303) 639-1224
e-mail: info@endoflifechoices.org
Web site: www.endoflifechoices.org

Working for increased choice in dying through legislation and lobbying, education, and patient advocacy, End-of-Life Choices publishes books, manuals, and newsletters on suicide, death, and dying, including *Final Exit*, a guide for those suffering with terminal illness and considering suicide. Being the oldest and the largest, it is the best known right-to-die organization in the United States.

Euthanasia Prevention Coalition BC
103-2609 Westview Dr., Suite 126, North Vancouver, BC V7N 4N2 Canada
(604) 794-3772 • fax: (604) 794-3960
e-mail: info@epc.bc.ca • Web site: www.epc.bc.ca

The coalition opposes the promotion or legalization of euthanasia and assisted suicide. It aims to educate the public on risks associated with the promotion of euthanasia and to increase public awareness as an advocate before the courts on issues of euthanasia and related subjects.

Euthanasia Research and Guidance Organization (ERGO)
24829 Norris Ln., Junction City, OR 97448-9559
(541) 998-1873
e-mail: ergo@efn.org • Web site: www.finalexit.org

The organization provides information and research on assisted death to the terminally ill who wish to end their suffering. It provides counseling to dying patients and develops ethical, psychological, and legal guidelines to help them and their physicians make end-of-life decisions. Publications include *Deciding to Die: What You Should Consider in Assisting a Patient to Die: A Guide for Physicians.*

Growth House, Inc.
(415) 863-3045
e-mail: info@growthhouse.org • Web site: www.growthhouse.org

Growth House seeks to improve the quality of compassionate care for the dying as an alternative to assisted suicide or euthanasia. It is engaged in public education and professional collaboration and provides resources to support groups, including a facility in San Francisco.

Hastings Center
21 Malcolm Gordon Rd., Garrison, NY 10524
(845) 424-4040
e-mail: mail@thehastingscenter.org
Web site: www.thehastingscenter.org

The center addresses fundamental ethical issues in health, medicine, and the environment, including euthanasia and physician-assisted suicide. Its publications include the *Hastings Center Report.*

Hospice Education Institute
3 Unity Square, PO Box 98, Machiasport, ME 04655-0098
(207) 255-8800 • fax: (207) 255-8008
e-mail: hospiceall@aol.com • Web site: www.hospiceworld.org

The institute teaches health care professionals and the public about hospice care and pain control for the terminally ill and works to improve end-of-life care.

Human Life International (HLI)
4 Family Life Ln., Front Royal, VA 22630
(540) 635-7884 • fax: (540) 636-7363
e-mail: hli@hli.org • Web site: www.hli.org

HLI rejects euthanasia and assisted suicide. It defends the rights of the unborn, the disabled, and those threatened by euthanasia, and it provides education, advocacy, and support services. It publishes the monthly newsletters *HLI Reports*, *HLI Update*, and *Deacons Circle*, as well as online articles on euthanasia.

International Anti-Euthanasia Task Force (IAETF)
PO Box 760, Steubenville, OH 43952
(740) 282-3810
e-mail: info@iaetf.org • Web site: www.iaetf.org

Opposing euthanasia, assisted suicide, and policies that threaten the lives of the medically vulnerable, IAETF works to influence the public, legislators, and the courts to ban euthanasia and assisted suicide. It publishes a newsletter, fact sheets, and position papers on euthanasia-related topics and files amicus curiae briefs in major "right-to-die" cases.

Last Acts Coalition
8618 Westwood Center Dr., Suite 315, Vienna, VA 22182
(703) 556-6800 • fax: (703) 556-4445
e-mail: lastacts@aol.com • Web site: www.lastacts.org

Last Acts is a campaign led by a coalition of professional and consumer organizations to improve end-of-life care. The organization promotes the campaign as an alternative to physician-assisted suicide.

National Hospice and Palliative Care Organization
(formerly the National Hospice Organization)
1700 Diagonal Rd., Suite 625, Alexandria, VA 22314
(703) 837-1500 • fax: (703) 837-1233
e-mail: info@nhpco.org • Web site: www.nho.org

Opposing euthanasia and assisted death, this organization educates the public about the benefits of hospice care for the terminally ill and their families. It promotes proper care and pain medication so that the dying can live out their lives comfortably, in the company of their families. It also educates and trains administrators and caregivers on hospice care and publishes the quarterlies *Hospice Journal* and *Hospice Magazine*, as well as books and monographs.

National Right to Life Committee (NRLC)
512 Tenth St. NW, Washington, DC 20004
(202) 626-8800
e-mail: nrlc@nrlc.org • Web site: www.nrlc.org

The committee is an activist group that opposes euthanasia and assisted suicide. It publishes the monthly *NRL News* and the four-part position paper "Why We Shouldn't Legalize Assisting Suicide."

Not Dead Yet
7521 Madison St., Forest Park, IL 60130
(708) 209-1500 • fax: (708) 209-1735
Web site: www.notdeadyet.org

This grassroots disability rights organization opposes the legalization of physician-assisted suicide and euthanasia on the grounds that the practice would harm disabled and chronically ill people.

Oregon Death with Dignity Legal Defense and Education Center
520 SW Sixth Ave., Suite 1030, Portland, OR 97204
(503) 228-4415 • fax: (503) 228-7454
e-mail: info@deathwithdignity.org • Web site: www.dwd.org

The center provides information, education, research, and support for a comprehensive range of end-of-life options, including physician-assisted suicide under certain conditions. It works to educate people about Oregon's Death with Dignity Act.

Partnership for Caring (formerly Choice in Dying)
1620 Eye St. NW, Suite 202, Washington DC 20006
(202) 296-8071 • fax: (202) 296-8352
e-mail: pfc@partnershipforcaring.org
Web site: www.partnershipforcaring.org

To improve communication about end-of-life decisions among the terminally ill, their loved ones, and health care professionals, Partnership for Caring provides education on the legal, ethical, and psychological consequences of assisted suicide and euthanasia. It publishes information materials on the various aspects of dying, including choices, advance directives, and dying at home.

Project on Death in America, Open Society Institute of Soros Foundation
400 W. Fifty-ninth St., New York, NY 10019
(212) 548-0600
e-mail: pdia@sorosny.org
Web site: www.soros.org/initiatives/pdia

The society works to transform the culture and experience of dying and bereavement through efforts in research, scholarship, the humanities, and the arts. It promotes reform in the provision of care, education, and public policy.

Right to Die Society of Canada
PO Box 39018, Victoria, BC V8V 4X8 Canada
(604) 386-3800 • fax: (604) 386-3800
e-mail: rights@freenet.victoria.bc.ca
Web site: www.ncf.davintech.ca/Freeport/social.services/rt-die/menu

Respecting the right of any terminally ill adult to choose his or her time and manner of death, the society helps patients through the dying process.

Scottish Voluntary Euthanasia Society (EXIT)
17 Hart St., Edinburgh EH1 3RN Scotland
(44) 131-556-4404
e-mail: vess@euthanasia.cc • Web site: www.euthanasia.cc

EXIT works to change British law in favor of individual patient choice, including physician-assisted suicide and euthanasia. It provides a variety of information and education materials on these subjects.

Voluntary Euthanasia Society
13 Prince of Wales Terr., London W8 5PG UK
(0171) 207-937-7770 • fax: (0171) 207-376-2648
e-mail: info@ves.org.uk • Web site: www.ves.org.uk

The society campaigns for the legalization of assisted dying for competent, incurably ill adults who request it, and it distributes advance directives.

For Further Research

Books

Christiaan Barnard, *Good Life, Good Death.* Englewood Cliffs, NJ: Prentice-Hall, 1980.

Margaret P. Battin, Rosamond Rhodes, and Anita Silvers, eds., *Physician Assisted Suicide: Expanding the Debate.* New York: Routledge, 1998.

Ian Dowbiggin, *A Merciful Life: The Euthanasia Movement in Modern America.* New York: Oxford University Press, 2003.

Ronald Dworkin, *Freedom's Law: The Moral Reading of the American Constitution.* Cambridge, MA: Harvard University Press, 1996.

Peter G. Filene, *A Cultural History of the Right-to-Die in America.* Chicago: Ivan R. Dee, 1998.

Kathleen Foley and Herbert Hendin, eds., *The Case Against Assisted Suicide: For the Right to End-of-Life Care.* Baltimore: Johns Hopkins University Press, 2002.

Maureen Harrison and Steve Gilbert, *Life, Death, and the Law: Landmark Right-to-Die Decisions.* San Diego: Excellent Books, 1997.

Derek Humphry, *Dying with Dignity: Understanding Euthanasia.* New York: Carol, 1992.

———, *Final Exit: The Practicalities of Self-Deliverance and Assisted Suicide for the Dying.* New York: Dell, 1996.

Derek Humphry and Ann Wickett, *The Right to Die: Understanding Euthanasia.* New York: Harper & Row, 1986.

Derek Humphry and Mary Clement, *Freedom to Die: People,*

Politics, and the Right-to-Die Movement. New York: St. Martin's, 1998.

Albert R. Jonsen, *A Short History of Medical Ethics.* New York: Oxford University Press, 2000.

John Keown, *Euthanasia, Ethics, and Public Policy: An Argument Against Legalisation.* Cambridge, UK: Cambridge University Press, 2002.

Gerald A. Larue, *Euthanasia and Religion: A Survey of Attitudes of World Religions to the Right-to-Die.* Los Angeles: Hemlock Society, 1985.

Jonathan D. Moreno, ed., *Arguing Euthanasia: The Controversy over Mercy Killing, Assisted Suicide, and the "Right to Die."* New York: Simon & Schuster, 1995.

Larry I. Palmer, *Endings and Beginnings: Law, Medicine, and Society in Assisted Life and Death.* Wesport, CT: Praeger, 2000.

M. Scott Peck, *Denial of the Soul: Spiritual and Medical Perspectives on Euthanasia and Mortality.* New York: Harmony Books, 1997.

Gregory E. Pence, *Classic Cases in Medical Ethics: Accounts of Cases That Have Shaped Medical Ethics, with Philosophical, Legal, and Historical Backgrounds.* New York: McGraw-Hill, 1995.

Carolyn S. Roberts and Martha Gorman, eds., *Euthanasia: A Reference Book.* Santa Barbara, CA: ABC-CLIO, 1996.

Francis A. Schaeffer and C. Everett Koop, *Whatever Happened to the Human Race?* Old Tappan, NJ: Fleming H. Revell, 1979.

Wesley J. Smith, *Culture of Death: The Assault of Medical Ethics in America.* San Francisco: Encounter Books, 2000.

Thomas Szasz, *Fatal Freedom: The Ethics and Politics of Suicide.* Westport, CT: Praeger, 1999.

Joni Eareckson Tada, *When Is It Right to Die? Suicide, Euthanasia, Suffering, Mercy.* Grand Rapids, MI: Zondervan, 1992.

James D. Torr, ed., *Euthanasia: Opposing Viewpoints.* San Diego: Greenhaven, 2000.

Michael M. Uhlmann, ed., *Last Rights? Assisted Suicide and Euthanasia Debated.* Grand Rapids, MI: Ethics and Public Policy Center and William B. Eerdmans, 1998.

Mary E. Williams, ed., *Terminal Illness: Opposing Viewpoints.* San Diego: Greenhaven, 2002.

Jerry B. Wilson, *Death by Decision: The Medical, Moral, and Legal Dilemmas of Euthanasia.* Philadelphia: Westminster, 1975.

Lisa Yount, *Physician-Assisted Suicide.* New York: Facts On File, 2000.

Marjorie Zucker, *The Right to Die Debate: A Documentary History.* Westport, CT: Greenwood, 1999.

Periodicals

Ad Hoc Committee of the Harvard Medical School to Examine the Definition of Brain Death, "A Definition of Irreversible Coma," *Journal of the American Medical Association*, August 5, 1968.

American Hospital Association, "A Patient's Bill of Rights, 1973," *Catalog No. 157758 of the American Hospital Association*, 1975.

John Cloud, "A Kinder, Gentler Death," *Time*, September 18, 2000.

Diane Coleman, "Assisted Suicide and Disability: Another Perspective," *Human Rights*, Winter 2000.

Ronald Dworkin, "Assisted Suicide: What the Court Really Said," *New York Review of Books*, vol. 44, no. 14, September 25, 1997.

Kathi Hamlon, "Prisoner Number 284797," *Human Life Review*, Summer 1999.

Frances M. Kamm, "A Right to Choose Death?" *Boston Review*, 1997.

Jack Kevorkian, "A Modern Inquisition," *Humanist*, November/December 1994.

Timothy E. Quill, "Death and Dignity—a Case of Individualized Decision Making," *New England Journal of Medicine*, March 7, 1991.

———, "Deciding About Death: Physician-Assisted Suicide and the Courts: A Panel Discussion," *Pharos*, Winter 1998.

Lawrence Rudden, "Death and the Law," *World & I*, May 2003.

John Shelby Spong, "In Defense of Assisted Suicide," *Human Quest*, May/June 1996.

Carl Wellmann, "A Legal Right to Physician-Assisted Suicide Defended," *Social Theory and Practice*, January 2003.

Internet Sources

Andrew I. Batavia and Hugh Gregory Gallagher, "Support for Right to Assisted Dying," *New Mobility Magazine*, August 2002. www.autonomy-now.org.

Lonnie R. Bristow, "Statement of the American Medical Association," April 29, 1996. www.house.gov.

CBS, "Oregon Assisted Suicide Upheld," *CBS News*, April 17, 2002. www.cbsnews.com.

Diane Coleman, "Acceptable Losses," *New Mobility Magazine*, August 2002. www.autonomy-now.org.

Hugh Gregory Gallagher, "'Slapping Up Spastics': The Persistence of Social Attitudes Toward People with Disabilities," *Issues in Law & Medicine*, Spring 1995. http://web2.infotrac.galegroup.com.

Richard Miniter, "The Dutch Way of Death," *Opinion Journal from the Wall Street Journal Editorial Page*, July 26, 2003. http://opinionjournal.com.

New York State Task Force on Life and the Law, "When Death Is Sought: Assisted Suicide and Euthanasia in the Medical Context," New York State Department of Health, October 2001. www.health.state.ny.us.

John Rawls et al., "Assisted Suicide: The Philosophers' Brief," *New York Review of Books*, March 27, 1997. www.nybooks.com.

William Rehnquist, "*Cruzan v. Director, Missouri Department of Health*," Legal Information Institute of Cornell Law School, 2003. www2.lawcornell.edu.

———, "*Dennis C. Vacco, Attorney General of New York et al., Petitioners v. Timothy E. Quill et al.*," Legal Information Institute of Cornell Law School, 2003. http://supct.law.cornell.edu.

Arjan Schippers, "Euthanasia," Radio Netherlands, July 23, 2001. www.nrw.nl.

Margaret Somerville, "The Case Against: Euthanasia and Physician-Assisted Suicide" *Free Inquiry*, Spring 2003. http://web4.infotrac.galegroup.com.

Sacred Congregation for the Doctrine of the Faith, "Declaration on Euthanasia," July 2003. www.vatican.va.

U.S. Holocaust Memorial Museum, "Mentally and Physically Handicapped: Victims of the Nazi Era," July 2003. www.ushmm.org.

Patient's Bill of Rights (American Hospital Association), 16
Patient Self-Determination Act (1990), 81, 135
People v. Kevorkian (1994), 107
Phaedo (Plato), 27–28, 30
Philbrick, Inez, 45
Philosopher's Brief (Dworkin et al.), 109, 136–37
physician-assisted suicide
  does not violate sanctity of life, 141–47
  is a transgression of divine sovereignty, 130–40
  is morally justified, 160–64
  in Netherlands, 125
    has resulted in deaths without consent, 148–59
    is a result of overemphasis on freedom/personal autonomy, 139
  opinion on, 203–204
    in 1937, 14
  risks of, 202
  should be option when palliative care fails, 196–204
  subverts role of doctors as healers, 176–84
    con, 168–75
  Supreme Court and, 19–20, 109–18
  vs. withdrawal of life support, 106–107, 180
Pius XII (pope), 15, 23–24, 56
  on passive euthanasia, 57, 58
Plato, 27–30, 33
Plum, Fred, 72
Potter, Charles Francis, 45, 47, 58, 60

privacy
  constitutional right to, in *Quinlan* case, 74–76
  as issue in right-to-die movement, 57
Pythagoreans, 27, 172

Quill, Timothy E., 104, 196
Quill v. Vacco (1997), 103, 131
Quinlan, Joseph, 74
Quinlan, Karen Ann, 16–17, 70–74
Quinlan case
  constitutional and legal issues in, 74–77
  right-to-die movement and, 16–17

Rachels, James, 136, 137
Rasmussen, Peter, 121
Rehnquist, William, 80, 103, 115, 121
  on due process clause, 91, 110–11
Reichleitner, Franz, 54
Reinhardt, Stephen, 188
Reno, Janet, 69
reproductive rights, link with euthanasia, 60–61
Republic (Plato), 28
right-to-die movement
  Derek Humphry's work in, 92–102
  Quinlan case and, 16–17
Roman Catholic Church, 15, 23–24, 61
  on intentional killing, 138
  on passive euthanasia, 58–60, 136
  view of, on death, 132–33
Rousseau, Jean-Jacques, 41
Rudden, Lawrence, 119